CONTEMPORARY SOCIOLOGY
Words _200 - 800_
Due _5/24/99_

EMPOWERMENT IN CHICAGO

Grassroots Participation
in Economic Development
and Poverty Alleviation

EMPOWERMENT IN CHICAGO

Grassroots Participation in Economic Development and Poverty Alleviation

Edited by

Cedric Herring
Michael Bennett
Doug Gills
Noah Temaner Jenkins

Great Cities Institute
University of Illinois at Chicago

Distributed by
University of Illinois Press
1998

Published by:
Great Cities Institute (MC 107)
University of Illinois at Chicago
322 S. Green Street, Suite 108
Chicago, IL 60607

Distributed by:
University of Illinois Press
Urbana and Chicago

Printed in the United States of America.
ISBN 0-9660180-0-1 (Paper)

Library of Congress Catalog Card Number Preassigned is 97-74989.

Main entry under title: *Empowerment in Chicago: Grassroots Participation in Economic Development and Poverty Alleviation.*

Includes bibliographic references.

Contents

Acknowledgements

The National Empowerment Zone Action Research Project has received significant financial support from two major foundations. The John D. and Catherine T. MacArthur Foundation funded our project for three years. The Joyce Foundation also contributed substantially to our first year of research. In addition, the MacArthur Foundation funded the research on which Chapter 7, by Nikolas Theodore, is based. The National Empowerment Zone Action Research Project also received financial and in-kind support from the University of Illinois at Chicago's Great Cities Institute, the Institute for Research on Race and Public Policy at UIC, and the Institute of Government and Public Affairs of the University of Illinois. We thank Wim Wiewel, Dean of the College of Urban Planning and Public Affairs; Lauri Alpern, Associate Director of the Great Cities Institute; and Robert F. Rich, former Director of the Institute of Government and Public Affairs. We also have had the backing of three UIC units: the Center for Urban Economic Development, the Department of Sociology, and the Jane Addams College of Social Work. We thank them for their support.

We would also like to thank participants in the Empowerment Zone process. Community residents, government officials, fellow researchers, activists from community-based organizations, and others in all of the cities in which we have conducted research have been helpful in our investigations. They have made sure that we have acquired important documents and access to their precious time. We have made use of their experiences and insights.

Also deserving of our gratitude are the members of our advisory committee: Professors Karla Hoff of the University of Maryland, Jody Kretzmann of Northwestern University, and Michael Dawson of the University of Chicago have provided us with valuable guidance.

We give thanks to Anthony Baker, Vernita A. Wickliffe-Lewis, Patricia O'Connor, Angela Agustin Mascareñas, Shelley Davis, Barbara Johnson, Tom Stribling, Cynthia Johnson, Jennifer Williams, Patrick Kaylor, Greg Washington, and Jean Templeton. These researchers have, in many cases, developed research projects around the Empowerment Zones and have shared their insights and written documents with us.

Finally, but certainly by no stretch of the imagination least, we thank Susan Motley, Program Officer for the Community Initiatives Program of the John D. and Catherine T. MacArthur Foundation and James Carlton, former Program Officer of the Joyce Foundation. Without their belief in our ability to make meaningful contributions to the Empowerment Zone process, this project simply would not have been possible.

Cedric Herring
Michael Bennett
Doug Gills
Noah Temaner Jenkins

Chapter 1

Empowerment in Chicago

Grassroots Participation in Economic Development and Poverty Alleviation

Michael Bennett, Noah Temaner Jenkins, and Cedric Herring

---

rban America faces formidable problems. Many observers are pessimistic about the outlook for America's urban centers, but others point to the historical role of cities in this country's economic, social, and cultural life and view such problems as far from insurmountable. The Clinton Administration's Community Empowerment Agenda is based on the optimistic premise that urban communities can generate opportunity and prosperity for their residents when they work in partnership with others. The idea of the Empowerment Zone (EZ) is based on the argument that community residents themselves must take the primary responsibility for their own fates. But the Empowerment Zone initiative also proposes that the federal government must become a more helpful supporter of families, businesses, and communities in their efforts to help themselves.

In January of 1994, the U.S. Department of Housing and Urban Development (HUD) published regulations for a national Empowerment Zone Demonstration Program. These Empowerment Zones provide each of six urban zones with $100 million in direct funding, in the form of Health and Human Services Title XX grants with flexibility in spending, along with various tax incentives and credits for businesses that are located in the designated zone and hire local residents. This legislation is intended to provide the means for reducing poverty in severely economically depressed areas by empowering community residents to create economic opportunity, sustainable communities, collaborative partnerships, and visions for social change. The expressed purpose of the program is to:

> empower American communities and their residents to create jobs and opportunity, take effective action to solve difficult and pressing economic, human, community and physical development challenges of today, and to build for tomorrow as part of a Federal-State-Local and private sector partnership. Businesses are to be encouraged to invest in distressed areas, thereby creating jobs, and comprehensive local strategic plans are to be adopted and implemented, furthering community development and assisting in the revitalization of these areas (*Federal Register* 1994: 59).

Despite the serious concerns about potential effects and effectiveness, the Empowerment Zone legislation is the most ambitious and most significant urban policy initiative to relieve distress in urban centers in more than 20 years.

Applicants to HUD were required to create a comprehensive strategic plan for the areas of their cities that they wished to become Empowerment Zones, and to demonstrate a commitment of public and private resources to address urban poverty, independent of successful designation. Each applicant had to demonstrate that its planning process and strategic plan complied with four principles:

1. Economic opportunity for impoverished residents, families, and communities;
2. Sustainable community development and capacity for building from within;
3. The building of partnerships; and
4. A vision of social change, including the building of new relationships between disadvantaged citizens and their government.

In *Empowerment in Chicago*, we examine Chicago's experience in the early stages of the Empowerment Zone process and provide an overview of the Empowerment Zone initiative as an economic development strategy. We present sociodemographic, quality of life, and citizen participation profiles of the neighborhoods involved in Chicago's Empowerment Zones and Enterprise Communities. We also trace the chronology of events and dates that have been important to the Empowerment Zone process, and provide key players' perceptions of events and developments that occurred in the initial stages of that process. In addition, we examine preliminary patterns in business growth and economic development in the zones as outcomes of the Empowerment Zone designation. Finally, we present the preliminary effects of zone designation on job growth, poverty alleviation, and changes in zone residents' access to jobs.

Although the contributors to this volume use different methodological and analytical tools, all of their works contribute to our understanding of the early stages of the Empowerment Zone process in Chicago. The authors address several empirical questions surrounding the Empowerment Zone process: what has gone right and what has gone wrong with the policy, how its implementation has differed from its original intent, and whom various actors perceive as winners and as losers.

Empowerment in Chicago makes several necessary additions to our understanding of the Empowerment Zone process in Chicago: (1) It expands the parameters of the discourse on this policy by looking beyond the economic effects of the issues. (2) It refines current arguments and makes them more specific by looking more closely at the contexts in which certain patterns do and do not hold true. (3) It makes possible the resolution of many of the current debates among those involved in the Empowerment Zone process, so that various formulations can be proposed and scrutinized. (4) It provides an opportunity for exchange among scholars, representatives from communities, policy makers, providers of technical assistance, and other persons interested in the Empowerment Zone process. (5) It provides systematic evidence on the nature and effects of the Empowerment Zone initiative in Chicago, and seeks to present such information in an accessible manner. (6) Finally, this book bridges gaps across disciplinary boundaries and crosses the lines between policy analysts and policy makers.

This introductory chapter serves two functions. First, it introduces the National Empowerment Zone Action Research Project and provides an overview of some of the controversies surrounding Empowerment Zones as spatially-based urban community development.

Second, this opening chapter fulfills a more traditional task. It provides a preview of the contributions to this volume.

The National Empowerment Zone Action Research Project

The National Empowerment Zone Action Research Project involves a multidisciplinary collection of scholars, staff members, and students at the University of Illinois at Chicago (UIC) and DePaul University. The faculty members on the research team are Michael Bennett, Doug Gills, and Cedric Herring. They hold appointments in the Egan Center at De Paul (Bennett), the Department of Sociology at UIC (Herring), the Center for Urban Economic Development at UIC (Gills), the College of Urban Planning and Public Affairs at UIC (Gills), the Institute of Government and Public Affairs of the University of Illinois (Herring), and the Institute for Research on Race and Public Policy at UIC (Herring).

The Project has been supported by the talents of a diverse core staff. Noah Temaner Jenkins, who has a master's degree in urban planning and policy with a specialization in economic development, is the project coordinator. Michelle Story-Stewart, a resident of an Empowerment Zone, is working toward her Ph.D. in public policy analysis. Kathy Feingold and Patricia O'Connor have both completed master's degrees in urban planning and policy. Javier Nogueras, a long-time community activist in Chicago's Latino Empowerment Zone area, was also part of the Project's support staff.

Other participants in the Project have included Anthony Baker, who recently received a Ph.D. in sociology from UIC; Vernita Wickliffe-Lewis, a Ph.D. candidate in public policy analysis at UIC; Angela Agustin Mascareñas, a doctoral student in sociology at UIC; and Shelley Davis, a master's student in urban planning and policy at UIC.

All of us are committed to community research in economic development and poverty alleviation. Together we have embarked on a project to monitor and influence the events associated with Empowerment Zones in nine cities: Atlanta, Baltimore, Camden, Chicago, Cleveland, Detroit, Los Angeles, New

York, and Philadelphia. We have worked to facilitate the Empowerment Zone process in these cities by providing policy makers and activists with information on events as they occur and with assessments of the planning and implementation processes.

In addition to the three principal investigators and our core staff, we have a number of Chicago collaborators. Among the contributors to this volume are John F. McDonald, professor of economics at the University of Illinois at Chicago, and Nikolas C. Theodore, project director for the Chicago Urban League.

We believe that research, to be most useful, should be comprehensive, informed by multiple perspectives, and implemented with guidance by those whose lives will be affected by the program being researched. That is, those who are to be affected by recommendations should be included in the process. Fortunately, our research team includes people who have been involved in the Empowerment Zone process in various capacities. We also plan to enhance our research by receiving input and guidance from knowledgeable members of the community at various stages of the research process.

We wish to address the following questions: (1) What are the prospects that the Empowerment Zone process can enhance citizens' involvement in governance, grassroots democratic participation, and the delivery of public services to residents? (2) How will these anticipated "bottom-up" participatory dynamics affect local leadership in cities and communities? (3) What new, innovative, and replicable social practices and organizational forms are likely to emerge as community-building strategies? and (4) How must the Empowerment Zone process be adjusted to increase the likelihood of achieving its goals in the implementing legislation?

One of the central purposes of the National Empowerment Zone Action Research Project is to review the Empowerment Zone/Enterprise Community application process to determine whether it truly represented the affected individuals in terms of access and outcome. As a demonstration project, the Empowerment Zone legislation will set the stage for much broader urban social policy. Although the Empowerment Zone program as a whole may not prove to be the solution to the deterioration of inner cities, certain elements of the legislation should prove crucial in reducing poverty and improving the residents' quality of life. Those who are committed to these urban areas must be informed of the results of this policy, and thus able to contribute to creating future policy.

Two additional objectives of this research are to examine the effects of this new legislation on citizen participation and to measure the economic development value of Empowerment Zones for residents and their communities. The uncommon approach of this policy makes it necessary to tailor research to measure effects accurately. In addition to traditional measures of community improvement such as employment, real estate values, business investment, and crime rates, we believe that the research findings must be measured against the standards of success that each city has set for itself.

The key to the success of the Empowerment Zone program seems to be the term *empowerment.* Are the residents of the Empowerment Zones becoming empowered to make changes in their communities? Empowerment in this case depends on the success of requirements for citizen participation and on attempts to "reinvent" government.

This project incorporates a mixture of traditional and nontraditional methods of data collection. These methods include interviews with participants at all levels, observations of public meetings, literature reviews, analyses of strategic plans and reports, workshops, focus groups, conferences, analysis of critical events, and quantitative analysis of census and survey data.

The research team has conducted interviews and focus groups with participants in the Empowerment Zone process from across the country. Our informants include public officials, representatives of community-based organizations, business representatives, and individual residents who participated in the Empowerment Zone planning process. The interviews and focus groups have emphasized the forms that citizen participation has taken in the planning and early implementation phases, along with individuals' perceptions of the strengths, weaknesses, and purposes of the legislation and its early implementation.

The research team has also reviewed and analyzed the strategic plans from the Empowerment Zone applications. We have tried to trace the content of these plans back to their original sources to determine whether ideas came directly from community residents, City Hall, business interests, or a combination of these. The team has also compared specific elements of the different plans. For example, we examined each of the eight plans' job development strategies. Later, we compared these plans with the actual implementation.

Critical events analysis is another important tool for understanding citizens' participation in the Empowerment Zone process. This methodology, which our research team developed, can be used to analyze and interpret data from specific events (e.g., community meetings, focus groups, the Empowerment Zone application process, and meetings of officially designated governing bodies), the content of official documents, and social surveys of community residents.

Critical events are consequential "turning points" or significant developments in a process, which predispose subsequent actions to follow identifiable lines. By definition, critical events provide qualitative change at a specific point in time, and limit the options for the outcomes. In studying political outcomes, one must understand the role of such critical events in limiting or expanding actors' range of choices. Critical events analysis is essentially an inductive research process: One begins with detailed observations about some political outcome or event and works backward to understand the conditions that led up to it. Critical events analysis can be used to inform discussions about the content of authentic democracy and how forms of citizen participation potentially influence who gains what from the Empowerment Zone process.

Our research team has also reviewed reports from designated Empowerment Zones to monitor progress. To ensure honest and comprehensive information, we have attempted to build a team of local informants in each city to supplement these reports. We recognize that different actors bring different perceptions, perspectives, and motivations to the assessment of implementation.

Scholars and activists across the nation are following the progress—and lack of progress—in cities struggling to realize the promises offered by this national Empowerment Zone program. *Empowerment in Chicago* is the first major publication based on the research of the National Empowerment Zone Action Research Project and related efforts. In this volume we examine Chicago's experience in the early phases of the Empowerment Zone process.

It seems fitting that our initial volume on Empowerment Zones looks at Chicago. Chicago is home to a school of sociology which, in the 1920s, defined a widely acknowledged method for identifying communities. It was also home to Mayors Richard J. Daley and Harold Washington, who, in their different ways, created nationally recognized political agendas for community development, and to Saul Alinsky, who launched an approach to organizing and empowering grassroots community residents worldwide.

Contributions to This Volume

windows of opportunity. p.16~

In December 1994, then-Secretary of HUD, Henry Cisneros, announced to Chicagoans that the federal Department of Housing and Urban Development had awarded the city one of six urban Empowerment Zone (EZ) designations. In the next chapter, Doug Gills and Wanda White place in historical context the efforts to enhance citizens' roles in planning, implementing, and evaluating federally funded development initiatives in Chicago. The authors describe the environmental conditions and outcomes that governments and citizens have experienced over the past five decades. They make use of interviews with participants in the Empowerment Zone process, official documents produced by various public and private entities involved in the process, and their own observations as participant-activists who were involved in the process in Chicago from the beginning. *Uneven quality in this chapter.*

In Chapter 3, Cedric Herring presents quantitative data from the U.S. Census and the Metropolitan Chicago Information Center surveys to show the degree of difference between EZ communities and other communities in the Chicago metropolitan area. He also presents data showing the degree to which EZ residents differ socially, politically, and economically from others in Chicagoland. Professor Herring compares people who live in communities that were designated as part of Chicago's Empowerment Zone with (1) residents of other low-income communities in Chicago that applied unsuc-

difference between Reagan/Bush and Clinton/Gore. p.21-22

cessfully for designation as Enterprise Communities; (2) residents of Chicago who live neither in the Empowerment Zone nor in any of the communities that applied to become Enterprise Communities; and (3) others who live in the metropolitan Chicago area but not in Chicago proper.

In Chapter 4, Noah Temaner Jenkins and Kathy Feingold summarize events that were important to the early phases of the Empowerment Zone process in Chicago. This brief contribution provides a basis for examining events, dates, and occasions that may be important to those who want to understand citizens' participation in the process.

Chapter 5, coauthored by Michelle Story-Stewart, Mark Sendzik, and Anna Marie Schuh, is a detailed, insightful analysis of the contents of Chicago's strategic plan and application. The authors examine the degree to which the final document contains ideas put forth by residents in the zone, either as individuals or through their organizations.

In Chapter 6, John McDonald considers the likely economic effects of the Empowerment Zone program. After a brief overview of the incentives for businesses provided by the Empowerment Zone legislation, he discusses the various economic and social goals of such initiatives. He presents findings which suggest that the Empowerment Zone program can lead to more efficient use of labor resources and to more equitable distribution of the proceeds of economic progress.

In Chapter 7, Nikolas Theodore examines the relationship between the regional economy and employment opportunities for inner-city residents. He analyzes the employment experiences and job search strategies of residents of Chicago's Empowerment Zone and compares them to the employment practices of businesses located in the zone. He concludes that firms in the zone have disincentives to provide job training to their employees; in addition, employees generally make fewer investments in training, and thus are at a disadvantage in the labor force. Still, with a large infusion of economic development resources, Empowerment Zones can be a much-needed catalyst for revitalization in economically depressed neighborhoods.

Finally, in Chapter 8, we hear the participants' own voices. In this chapter Michael Bennett and Javier Nogueras present interviews with Rosanna Marquez and Sherry Rontos, two key figures in the EZ process. These interviews offer firsthand accounts of events and developments during the planning and application phase. Ms. Marquez was Mayor Richard M. Daley's key liaison during the early stages of the process; Ms. Rontos is a community activist in one of the three geographic areas in the zone.

As policy aimed at alleviating poverty, the success of Empowerment Zone legislation will be determined by the opportunities it provides to low-income individuals. We hope to see improved educational and economic opportunities, increased resources that allow individuals the opportunity to make choices, and an overall improvement in quality of life. Without such outcomes, economic development cannot be considered a success. We wish to determine whether the new policy is having these desired effects on individual lives.

We have been engaged in dialogue not only with fellow scholars, but also with policy analysts, policy makers, and members of the community interested in the links between government policy and economic development. These exchanges have been accomplished through (1) discussion of our research with key informants and focus groups selected from various community groups and neighborhoods in the Chicago metropolitan area, (2) the presentation of our preliminary findings at workshops and colloquia, (3) the presentation of findings at professional and policy conferences; (4) the publication of a newsletter and occasional reports; (5) the publication of scholarly articles and other material directed toward those with technical expertise and familiarity with the subject matter; and (6) the publication of less technically oriented works such as this edited volume. These strategies will ensure that our findings are broadcast to persons both inside and outside academia who are interested in economic development. We offer this volume in that spirit.

We hope that *Empowerment in Chicago* will be useful to urban planners, sociologists, political scientists, journalists, government officials, public administrators, policy analysts, students, community activists, and others who are interested in place-based development strategies, public policy, and the form and content of citizens' participation in these initiatives.

disadvantages/limitatoins
— not a theoretically informed
analysis.

Chapter 2

Community Involvement in Chicago's Empowerment Zone

Doug Gills and Wanda White

T he story of Chicago's Empowerment Zone should be recorded for use by analysts in urban planning as well as social science researchers and community development practitioners. These groups may find rich lessons in the Empowerment Zone process, particularly as it relates to collaborative research and what we term citizen or community participation. We want these lessons to reach broader audiences than the typical academic readership, and hope that social and community development practitioners will share them with their constituents. Moreover, we hope policy analysts will incorporate our findings on the development of the Empowerment Zone initiative into their policy designs and will convey their recommendations to policy makers, to civic organizations, institutions, and social advocacy networks seeking to influence public policy.

We focus on what can be termed citizen involvement or community participation as one of the features of the federal Empowerment Zone initiative. We move from the local level through the various levels of partnership building, including the municipalities, the affected states, and the intergovernmental federal agencies. We also articulate social and community development objectives with the various aspects of the policy formation process.[1]

We are most concerned with articulating collaborative, participatory research with the broader collaborative practices of the various partners in developing the Empowerment Zone structures and processes at the local and national levels. Collaborative research will contribute greatly to the development of the Empowerment Zone process. In this report, the term collaborative, participatory research is synonymous with what we call social action (or applied) research. In such research the academic scientist's tools and techniques are adapted to social problem solving and inquiry with immediate, real-world, policy outcomes and/or political consequences.

Currently, at best, we can only make certain inferences about what these outcomes might be. We do so by linking what Empowerment Zone participants suggest is their intent with the federally sanctioned, stated goals and objectives of the initiative (as set forth by the federal crafters of the legislation and regulations). Moreover, we can base our assessments on the relationship between what was proposed by Empowerment Zone participants in cities such as Chicago, as they sought designation, with their degree of success in accomplishing the legislative and regulatory aims of the Empowerment Zone process. On the basis of our analysis of these practices, we can offer useful conclusions about current implementation and interactions of the collaborating partners in Empowerment Zone cities. Also, through reviewing this process, we can assess the future effectiveness of this initiative, particularly as it relates to community and citizen participation. We focus on developments in Chicago, but our findings will have implications for other cities where the EZ process is being applied.

We use interviews with participants, and we incorporate official documents produced by public and private entities connected with the Empowerment Zone process at the federal, state, and local levels. We combine this material with our own observations as participant-activists in the process from its inception. We also supplement interviews with secondary materials and with accounts of the historical antecedents of the Empowerment Zone process.

We believe that the Empowerment Zone initiative is likely to be more significant at the local levels of the policy development process than at the national level, and that it creates significant windows of opportunity[2] for activists at both ends of the policy reform spectrum. We also believe that the modes of interaction required in the Empowerment Zone process offer opportunities to advance collaborative research and action between academicians, policy advocates, and community activists. All of these individuals, working together, can create or press for reforms that facilitate the extension of democracy and development. It can do so through collective work to alleviate poverty at community, family, and individual levels of intervention. In this respect, our research approach is consistent with the social action research model.[3]

Before we examine the history and current state of Empowerment Zone implementation in cities such as Chicago, we offer some background on the Empowerment Zone concept.

Background

The Empowerment Zone Initiative was established as a pilot urban policy demonstration initiative of the Clinton-Gore administration. It became law as part of the Omnibus Budget Reconsolidation Act of 1993, passed by Congress in September 1993. Under this legislation, the U.S. Department of Housing and Urban Development (HUD) was designated as the lead agency to coordinate the Empowerment Zone initiative through an interagency task force. This task force combined the urban programs of several federal departments and intergovernmental agencies.

Because the initiative was linked to the Clinton-Gore move to streamline government spending and to avert government waste of resources, the Community Enterprise Development Board was established under the Office of the Vice-President. This Board articulated with the administration's campaign to "reinvent government" in at least two ways. The first was to make government more efficient and more accessible, moving it closer to the people while cutting through the duplication of effort that is common in federal departments. Second, it attempted to ensure that government would become more accessible to the people at the local level. It would become more responsive to the needs of local communities by fostering greater collaboration between government entities at all levels, the community nonprofit service and development sector, and businesses. It would encourage reinvestment in central cities to address the persistent poverty and neglect of individuals, families, and distressed communities. The legislation also provided for at least three rural Empowerment Zones to target persistent rural poverty. Here, however, we are concerned with the urban EZ process.

The Empowerment Zone legislation, as passed by Congress, was predicated on four major principles:

◆ The addressing of individual, family, and community impoverishment by creating economic opportunities for Empowerment Zone residents and for marginalized businesses owned by Empowerment Zone residents, thus producing incentives for businesses as well as for residents of designated EZs;

◆ The pursuit of sustainable communities so as to create enduring viability resulting from the infusion of government resources and private-sector reinvestment, coupled with community innovation, creativity, and collective efforts addressing the causes of economic distress and impoverishment;

♦ The creation of sustained partnerships between business, government, and the organized community agents, in which true grassroots participation would be sustained throughout the process; and

♦ A strategic vision of social change addressing the sources of poverty and altering the way government does business with its citizens, such that basic relations between the people and public authorities could be described as "reinvented."

The Empowerment Zone partnership applicants were committed to demonstrate these goals within a 10-year implementation period, whether or not HUD granted designation as an Empowerment Zone. Designated partnerships would receive $100 million in HHS Social Services Block Grant (Title XX) funds to be administered by HUD through the states over a two-year period. These funds could be used to attract other public and private money to be invested in the targeted Empowerment Zone communities.

In addition, the designated EZs would be eligible to receive up to $500 million in Economic Development Initiative (EDI) funds to support business enterprise development. Businesses located in the EZs would be eligible to receive income tax credits of up to $3,000 per each hired employee who maintained residence in the designated EZs. In addition, they could receive other tax credits for capital investments and certain kinds of inventory purchases in businesses located in the Empowerment Zone which employed Empowerment Zone residents as workers.

Funds would be released to EZ-designated partnerships when the Empowerment Zone designee met the HUD and HHS benchmarks and assurance requirements, and executed the final Letter of Agreement/Memorandum of Agreement. The agreement included the assurances that goals and governance requirements, as affirmed in the original HUD application submission containing the Empowerment Zone partnership's Strategic Plan, were in place. Noncompliance with the "certifications" (conditions and agreed upon terms) in the application could result in revocation of Empowerment Zone designation.

The Empowerment Zone process is rooted in community economic development and human (resources) development movements of the past two decades. These two areas are aspects of the more encompassing community development movement, which is most evident at the local or municipal level of public policy formation. Well before 1993, however, this movement had developed a considerable national network of individuals and organizations capable of acting collectively to influence federal- and state-level public policy formation.

In Chicago, this movement and its components have acquired a reputation for sophistication and resource capability. The participants laid the development policy foundation for the Harold Washington mayoralty, and the movement was important in Washington's election in 1983. Since Washington's untimely death in 1987, the community-based development movement, in combination with the organized struggle for community empowerment, has been attacked incessantly by the resurgent Democratic Party machine and the new urban growth consortium in the city.[4]

Differences between the Empowerment Zone and Previous Urban Policy Initiatives

Some significant differences exist between the Empowerment Zone Initiative and previous federal urban policy initiatives, including the Federal and State Enterprise Zone program established under the Reagan-Bush administrations (1981-1993). The Reagan-Bush initiative had two major components, the Enterprise Zones and the Job Training Partnership Act, which established private industry councils at state and local levels. The Reagan-Bush enterprise zone program offered incentives in the form of tax credits to businesses in the targeted industrial areas, but extended no direct benefits to the residents of those areas.

The Reagan-Bush program included no direct, citizen-based participation except by government-appointed private industry councils. There were no requirements for sustained collaborations between government, business, and community-based participants in the targeted areas. The program did not provide for targeted communities' participation in the planning, implementation, monitoring, and assessment of the program; nor did it include any direct social service, human and community resource, or capacity-building components.

The Clinton-Gore initiative, which we call the Empowerment Zone, is unique in that it has fused elements of the Reagan-Bush initiative with a community development orientation. It promotes the linkage between the empowerment of community-level constituencies and their needs for comprehensive development activities, addressing poverty and socio-economic distress at the individual, family, and community levels. This initiative embraces the notion that impoverished members of distressed communities will have opportunities to move out of poverty. They will be able to participate in independent collective action, in viable collaborations, and in public policy decisions taken to improve their lives. At its best, the Empowerment Zone concept has a conservative philosophic framework and a relatively progressive rhetoric.

This initiative is conservative in its acknowledgment that members of the private, corporate sector must be given incentives to invest in the central-city communities where poor, unemployed individuals and families are concentrated. It is conservative insofar as it does not reject the supply-side economic approach that was embraced by the Reagan-Bush administration. At the same time, it rejects the idea that supply-side incentives ever created benefits that trickled down to the residents of distressed communities in the form of jobs, enhanced marketable skills, and the like.

The Clinton-Gore Empowerment Zone initiative also does not accept the conservative view that poverty is due to lack of motivation among the impoverished. That is, this policy orientation does not blame the victims for their condition. Yet, at the same time, they are not absolved of responsibility for removing themselves from distress through concerted actions at the individual, family, and community levels, especially after economic opportunities have been identified. Furthermore, the Clinton-Gore Empowerment Zone concept provides direct resources to address poverty and alienation at these levels. It also increases the program's chances for success by insisting on sustained government, business, and community partnerships and on area residents' continued involvement in designing and implementing solutions to the problems at hand. While funded for two years, the partnerships are to be sustained by local resources for ten years.

The leading characteristic of the Clinton-Gore Empowerment Zone initiative is that it combines the conservative economists' "enterprise" and "zone" concepts with the communitarian and populist sociopolitical concepts of "community" and "empowerment." Under Reagan-Bush, supply-side economic incentives targeted industry-based businesses.

Under Clinton-Gore, incentives are targeted to resident-based impact areas, namely enterprise communities and empowerment zones. The Empowerment Zone concept is an eclectic initiative that contains features from both ends of the political spectrum. Its conservatism is apparent to all who investigated the enterprise zone initiative under the Reagan-Bush administrations. Less obvious is its tenacious liberalism: It creates individual-oriented economic opportunities and benefits while embracing certain radical-sounding tenets of communitarianism and urban populism.

Benefits are available to individual residents, constituents, businesses, and families; however, they are tied to community building and to developing sustainable communities. Thus, the most distinctive trait of the Empowerment Zone initiative is the notion of community empowerment through facilitating ordinary citizen activists' involvement in policy making. President Bush proposed a class-biased, voluntarist, "Thousand Points of Light" notion of citizen participation. In contrast, Clinton and Gore recognize that just as businesses need incentives to invest in the inner cities, economically distressed individuals and families need incentives to alleviate poverty and to remain in developing communities, if personal and community assets are to accumulate.

national and local community action organizations,

Goals of the Federal Empowerment Zone Process

The Empowerment Zone initiative was advanced by the new Clinton-Gore administration in a socioeconomic and political context. The turn toward right-wing conservatism of the late 1970s and early 1980s had been consolidated into U.S. politics by the 1992 presidential elections. Congress was becoming much more conservative, even though at least nominally it remained under Democratic Party control. The Republicans gained control after the 1994 congressional elections. Clinton won the 1992 presidential election by a plurality, not by a majority. His victory was possible only because the Republicans were divided by conservative candidates and by Ross Perot's candidacy. Although Clinton won majorities in major cities, he did not advance a coherent urban/domestic agenda during his campaign. He had tacitly endorsed the Reagan-Bush enterprise zone program.

A number of sociopolitical developments during the presidential campaign and early in the Clinton presidency facilitated the promotion of the Empowerment Zone concept: (1) the downturn in the U.S. economy, in which unemployment reached an all-time non-Depression high. Although corporate profits soared, investments were not made in industrial infrastructure and in job-generation in the manufacturing sector of the economy; (2) the Rodney King verdict, in which Los Angeles police officers were absolved of charges of excessive force and brutality, sparked violence among some people of color in Los Angeles and several other cities across the United States; and (3) the Perot campaign and movement, which opened up the national political and public policy process. President Clinton needed an effective, politically marketable urban program. Such an important, if symbolic, gesture would increase the new administration's credibility.

The urban crisis has at least four significant dimensions: economic, fiscal, political, and social. It was thought that major cities needed a stimulant to jolt them out of crisis. The new administration offered a token appropriation of $2.5 billion over the next two fiscal years while buying some time. It was hoped that the structuring of the EZ as a national competition would facilitate a massive mobilization in the central cities, which would change the local and national political climate. Moreover, it was hoped that the national demonstration would work well enough to justify a new, full-fledged national urban development policy with adequate funding.

The community economic development approach was combined with the community empowerment model. The latter was based on notions of community control, self-determination, and decentralization of public institutions. This fusion approach was palatable to Republicans as well as to conservative Democrats. Moreover, it was compatible with Perot supporters' concern about social and capital reinvestment in American industrial development. Lacking any other viable urban economic and industrial development policy and confronting fierce opposition to his health insurance, welfare, and education access packages, Clinton was desperate to build support in the heavily populated urban centers. Thus, the Clinton-Gore administration was amenable to the aggressive advances by community and human resource development advocates. The administration hoped that proponents could agree on a new, more comprehensive approach to poverty, which did not appear to give handouts to welfare recipients and the interests surrounding the welfare services industry. If this was achieved, perhaps a national urban economic development policy could be crafted. Such a policy could be pursued if it did not cost too much.

By the summer of 1993, community services and community development proponents had worked out the basic concept and language of a new urban policy. Yet, this initiative still had to be sold to a reluctant Congress. In the fall, sufficient numbers of the (then) Democratic majority won over moderate Republicans on the grounds that the Empowerment Zone concept was a demonstration program. It would be a competitive nonentitlement program in which communities were selected on the basis of merit. Only a few cities would be designated, although many would be eligible to apply.[6]

How the Chicago Empowerment Zone Process Began

In Chicago, various networks of community development and community services organizations have developed over the past two decades. Most of these networks are directed by nonprofit, community-based organizations (CBOs). Since the early 1980s, beginning under Mayor Jane Byrne's administration and continuing with aggressive support under Mayor Harold Washington, these networks have evolved into stable, multiracial, and multinational coalitions. Most of these coalitions targeted low-income communities for redevelopment and sought to provide increased technical assistance and organizational skills enhancement to low-income residents and the constituents of CBOs. By the end of the 1980s, these organizations had established links to national networks and associations of community development and community service providers. Their members held positions of technical expertise and served professionally as development practitioners in community-based organizations.

The concept of community-directed development and groups advocating community economic development (CED) [7] are most fully developed in Chicago. Community groups in Chicago also have raised the concept and practice of community empowerment to a high level, as well as the related notions of community building and capacity building. Although larger and more progressively successful groups elsewhere may pursue some aspect of community development, Chicago historically has been in the vanguard of this movement. Its housing, economic, and employment development coalitions have served as models for groups of activists in other cities.

This tradition exists, in part, because Chicago has always been a city of neighborhoods—neighborhoods organized around a collective ethnic, nationality, racial, and/or class identity. The modern [8] neighborhood development movement was based on the independent community-based

25

organization movement, which originated in the civil rights, black power, and antipatronage movements of the 1960s and 1970s. Its development continued into the 1990s, in spite of frequent digressions into parochialism and separatist trends, notions of "turf," and the niches that various associations had carved out for themselves. Coalitions have been a distinctive and pervasive, if not dominant, feature of Chicago's community politics and public policy arena, particularly over the past 20 years. There are about a dozen stable coalitions in Chicago that are dominated by community-based organizations.

An impetus for community coalition building was the reaction of community-based, labor-related, and populist activists to the Reagan-era budget cuts. Community-based groups united to protect the gains made over the previous 15 to 20 years in the community development and community services movement. They also led and supported constituency-based struggles against the Reagan retrenchment on social services and welfare state programs. Finally, both the CED and the human resource development movements were accelerated under the favorable conditions of Harold Washington's mayoralty in Chicago. Washington had campaigned on positions favoring the reproduction of the community-based development movement. His campaign earned the support of the community activists in development and human services, who, in turn, gave him access to their constituents.[9]

Although the production of CED may have been quantitatively modest, it has unquestionably influenced urban and now national policy. Abundant practical experience and innovativeness have emerged from the community development movement and the activities of its practitioners, most of whom were grassroots citizen activists until the late 1980s. Only in this most recent period have academically trained urban and community planners, along with economic development specialists, become prominent in community development organizations.

Thus, the legitimacy of community economic and human services development has been assured, at least for the immediate future. Academic research departments increasingly are incorporating community development courses into their curricula and their allied urban studies programs.

The value of an organic, experiential connection to community-based practice among the students of urban planning and policy development has become clear to academic people. Every year, more community placement opportunities become available to academically trained and skilled graduates. In this connection, the Policy Research and Action Group (PRAG) established the graduate internship placement program several years ago. Recently, it has developed a community apprenticeship program. The collaboration is a two-way process: Community development organizations benefit in turn from the technical, organizational, and policy-analytic skills that academically trained personnel apply to issues - facing communities and their constituents. For this reason, community groups have insisted that research centers offer grassroots activists more opportunities to enter the academy to acquire advance social problem-solving and research skills. In the struggles surrounding implementation of the Empowerment Zone process at the local level, we have seen the practical value of the cross-fertilization between academy and community.

Roots of the Empowerment Zone Concept

In December 1992, Tim Wright, an attorney and former commissioner of the Department of Economic Development under Mayor Eugene Sawyer (1987-1989), was appointed as a liaison to a Clinton Transition Team task force on economic development and infrastructure. Wright approached the authors about whether CWED and the University of Illinois Center for Urban Economic Development

(UICUED) could facilitate a meeting of scholar activists and human and community development practitioners in Chicago.

The purpose of the conference was to provide input into the Clinton-Gore transition. The organizing issue was posed as follows: If the Clinton Administration was unable to increase funding to support urban social, economic, and human services programs and job-generating projects, especially during the first two years, what regulatory and administrative changes could be made in existing programs that would make it easier to serve constituents and recipients? Could waivers be granted? Could there be greater articulation between federal agencies? Could ways found be to increase the involvement of community practitioners and constituents in planning and implementing the existing federal programs targeting inner-city areas such as those in Chicago?

The project was undertaken collaboratively by Wanda White, then policy director at the Women's Self Employment Project; Luther Snow, then Executive Director at CWED; Wim Wiewel, then Director of UICUED; and Doug Gills, who was a faculty member at UICUED and was Deputy Director, on leave, at the Kenwood Oakland Community Organization. Some 40 community and economic development activists, human services practitioners, and social action researchers met at UICUED in late December 1992.

At the conference, after reviewing the charge to the group, the participants divided into work groups on housing and homelessness, economic and employment development, health and human services, and infrastructure. Coordinators were appointed for each group. The groups were assigned to meet and draft brief policy papers that would undergo review and synthesis at the next meeting, to be held in early January 1993. The groups met during the holidays and brought in other key persons; they generated draft briefing papers, which were distributed during the first week of January.

The task force met again in mid-January. The initial drafts were modified, final formatting was agreed upon, and the edited product was delivered to Tim Wright. In the third week in January copies were sent to Henry Cisneros, the HUD Secretary-designate, and to each member of the Illinois-Chicago Congressional delegation, before the Clinton-Gore inauguration.

Similar work groups were established in other cities as well. At that time we did not know that this work would give rise to a series of conferences in Arkansas and in Washington. We did not know that it would lead to a rethinking of federal urban development policies and practices, especially regarding the relationship between central cities and urban communities, on one hand, and the federal government, on the other. During the late spring and summer of 1993, several national economic and community development force meetings were held, involving human services activists, community and economic development practitioners, and the Clinton-Gore transition and early governance organization. These meetings included people from Chicago and other cities who had taken part in the original winter meetings initiated by Tim Wright.

Many of the ideas that were contained in the winter task force meetings in Chicago found their way into the Clinton-Gore urban and domestic development agenda. These ideas applied not only to the Empowerment Zone but also to the Clinton-Gore White House proposals for restructuring federal government. One of these ideas centered around what is now known as the Consolidated Plan (Con-Plan). The aim of this plan is the creation of a coordinated interagency "continuum of care" to govern delivery of services to local urban constituents (what might be called "comprehensive service delivery") as well as interlinked agency coordination.

The other aspect of Con-Plan, and perhaps its most common expression, is the requirement that lead agencies receiving community service and community development block grants, housing grants, and other funds for economic development must create a comprehensive strategic plan. This plan must involve broad community participation in its development, implementation, oversight, and assessment. Moreover, Con-Plan stipulated that municipalities would no longer develop as many as seven or eight applications a year for various city-administered programs. Instead, beginning in January 1995, these applications would be consolidated into a single comprehensive application.

These critical ideas, which are found in the Empowerment Zone and the Con-Plan concepts, were anticipated by community development work in Chicago and certainly other cities. They included the following:

- The notion of community directed development, whereby citizen constituents control the process of redevelopment and participate in the planning and development process as equals with the private and public sector; the notion of multidimensional accountability, whereby the service recipients as well as the service providers (public or private) are reciprocally held accountable;

- The principle that comprehensive and multifaceted service supports must be present to address the problems of poverty, economic and social distress, and alienation;

- The notion that the object of comprehensive support services is not to maintain impoverishment but to reduce poverty through commitment to a vision of social change that addresses the systemic causes of poverty and social distress;

- The principle that ongoing community and citizens' participation is extended throughout all aspects of the policy development process—

planning (design), implementation, monitoring/oversight as well as assessment;

- The idea of sustained collaborative partnership to address systemic problems;
- The idea that poverty cannot be alleviated without asset accumulation at the individual, family, and community levels;
- The notion that shared power is the outcome of the demand for community empowerment (HUD 1994).

Chicago social action researchers, scholar-activists, and community-based practitioners could respond so quickly and decisively to the opportunity presented by the Clinton-Gore administration because a number of networks, collaborations, community-based coalitions, and partnerships already existed. These formations provided opportunities for scholars, researchers, and practitioners to meet, exchange ideas, and work through problems together. They learned to speak each other's language.

One such setting for these lessons is the Policy Research and Action Group (PRAG). Founded in 1990, the PRAG is a consortium of universities, agencies providing technical assistance, and representatives of community-based organizations. The themes underlying the work of most of the formations are also central to the Empowerment Zone concept: community empowerment, community-directed development, and comprehensive human and social-economic development services to individuals, families, and communities.

Other coalitions and associations also created opportunities for community-oriented researchers and community practitioners to come together. These included: the Chicago Association of Neighborhood Development Organizations (CANDO), CWED, UICUED, and the Northwestern University Center for Urban Policy and Public Affairs.

Coalitions such as the Chicago Rehab Network, the Chicago Jobs Council, and the Neighborhood Capital Budget Group have held forums that facilitated dialogue and social action between scholars, activists, researchers, and practitioners. In addition, more long-established civic and civil rights advocacy groups such as the Chicago Urban League, the Community Renewal Society, the United Way of Chicago, the Latino Institute, and the Jewish Council on Urban Affairs have conducted forums on this subject.

More recently, the Donors' Forum and some of its associated foundations have facilitated such dialogues and collaborations. In fact, the Policy Research Action Group began in 1988-1989 as a result of a day-long conference among these groups. (This meeting was sponsored by the MacArthur Foundation.) It was convened in response to the "McCarron series" of articles on urban economic development, published in the Chicago Tribune. These articles were tantamount to Martin Luther's "95 Theses": John McCarron, apparently the voice of the new urban growth coalition in Chicago, issued a manifesto on the new "Protestant (urban development) reformation." McCarron launched a sustained, vicious attack directed at the community development movement in the city; he characterized the movement as "anti-development," impeding residential and commercial redevelopment, especially in low-income communities. (The current administration in City Hall, led by Mayor Richard M. Daley, appears to be carrying out the new urban development program on behalf of the city's growth coalition.[10]

In addition to the launching of PRAG, this conference led to the production of *Challenging Uneven Development: Toward an Urban Agenda for the 1990s*, by Phil Nyden and Wim Wiewel. It was a widely distributed edited volume of commissioned articles that described the scope and content, the challenges and opportunities, the limitations and potentialities of the Chicago community development movement. This book served as a framework and acknowledged the central role of a movement that is based on collaboration between activist-minded researchers and applied research-minded community development practitioners.

Because of these collaborative networks and community-based coalitions, Chicago was able to mobilize for the Empowerment Zone application process and to give the HUD application its progressive character and content. In Chicago this document is known as the *Chicago Empowerment Zone Strategic Plan* (Chicago Public Library, 1994).

In the most recent dialogue and struggles concerning the Empowerment Zone, the overall community development movement, which includes human service, social support, and development groups, has come to appreciate the need for a common language of public policy discourse. Only recently, for example, have we come to realize that terms such as CED, holistic development, continuum of care, and comprehensive community development have the same meaning, particularly from the standpoint of service recipients and community constituents. That common language embodies understandings of activists, applied researchers, and policy analysts as well as those of the community constituents, and these understandings are reflected in the Chicago Empowerment Zone Strategic Plan.[11]

The Role of CWED as a Coalition

From its inception in 1982, the Community Workshop on Economic Development (CWED) has been a collaboration between community and urban economic development practitioners, social action researchers, and scholar-activists interested in applied urban economic development and policy. However, it is the community-based organization leadership which drives the coalition.

CWED's history was rooted in the older community organization-based coalition that led to the formation of the Chicago Rehab Network. That group was organized in the mid-1970s as a coalition of nonprofit agencies for housing rehabilitation and repair and for affordable housing advocacy, who united in their opposition to gentrification and shelter displacement in underdeveloped neighborhoods.

By the early 1980s, the low-income housing movement had expanded to absorb other issues related to neighborhood and urban economic development. In 1981-1982, there were divisions of emphasis in the shelter rehabilitation and the emerging community development arena among groups who identified themselves in various ways: as focused on housing, as involved in economic employment enterprise development and industrial attraction and retention, and as multifaceted community development organizations. In this friendly context the latter groups fused with social action researchers and academic applied economists to form CWED.

CWED focused on two major issues. First, the group concentrated on the impacts, the challenges, and even the potential opportunities resulting from Reagan-Bush programs designed ostensibly to generate economic recovery for industrial urban centers. These included the Enterprise Zone and the Job Training Partnership Act; the latter replaced the more effective Comprehensive Education and Training Act (CETA) programs begun under President Carter. The Reagan Administration established the Private Industry Council (PIC).

Second, CWED criticized Mayor Jane Byrne's redefinition of Chicago as a "world class city" to be based on entertainment, convention centers, sports complexes, tourism, and high-tech industries, with a low-paid, service-based employment sector. CWED activists believed there were alternatives to triaging the neighborhoods and writing off scores of poor community areas while concentrating public and private investments in the central business district and the expansion of the O'Hare Airport region.

The proposed 1992 World's Fair served as a catalyst for a community economic development agenda in Chicago. Mayor Byrne had sought aggressively to have Chicago chosen as the site for the Fair. The Fair had the support of the financial, real estate, and corporate business sectors in Chicago. Its centerpieces were the (then) proposed expansion of the McCormick Place exposition complex in Chicago near the South Side lake front, a domed, multiplex stadium as the future home of the Chicago Bears, and the rerouting of Lake Shore Drive. The project also included the acquisition of lands as far south as 35th Street and as far west as Halsted Street, to provide housing, parking, and exposition-related facilities for the national pavilions.

The accommodation of national pavilions, however, was not the greatest concern to critics of the Fair. The issue was: what would happen to the existing residents and businesses? Many saw in the Fair proposal a drive for economic development that would lead to the wholesale displacement of poor blacks and Latinos from the near South Side lake front.

According to critics such as Lew Krienberg, a leading policy analyst and organizer with the Jewish Council on Urban Affairs, the main force behind the Fair was the same dynamic as promoted the "Chicago 21" plan. The plan was to redevelop the south Loop and near South Side lake front by displacing poor residents and the industrial belt that rings the Loop commercial district, using public resources to pay for real estate property. That plan was firmly resisted by community activists, who mobilized in the emergent Latino community as well as the African-American neighborhoods. For the first time, in 1977-1979, a multiracial, multinational social movement was organized around urban and community economic development policy issues.

Activists such as Krienberg and Walter "Slim" Coleman, editor of the radical populist *All Chicago City News*, argued perceptively that the major difference between the older Chicago 21 Plan and the newer Fair Plan was that the latter was packaged around an international party and cultural exhibition. Both were displacement strategies. In both plans, the public taxpayers were to pay for land and property acquisition. This perhaps was the defining feature of the new development growth consortium in Chicago. This consortium consisted primarily of the real estate and construction industry, the mortgage banking industry, and the supporting legal and building design firms.[12]

In addition, the Fair's developers and investors wanted the public to underwrite the expenditures of the Fair Commission, thus guaranteeing profits for the investors. Finally, the Fair developers would profit from the hundreds of millions of dollars in pre-Fair infrastructure development for post-Fair investment in large-scale residential development. Krienberg asserted that Commonwealth Edison, Chicago's electric power company, was a prime supporter of the Fair because it would be virtually assured that the post-Fair residential development would attract as many as 250,000 to 350,000 new residents into Chicago's new, upscale area on the lake front.[13]

Like her successor, current Mayor Richard M. Daley, Mayor Byrne sought to rebuild the city's tax base on the basis of increasing home ownership. In this strategy, first-time home buyers are targeted as recipients of low-interest loans and a significant share of the middle class is lured back into the central city from Chicago's burgeoning suburbs. The enticements are cultural and entertainment amenities, insulation from the urban poor in the black and Latino neighborhoods near the target redevelopment area, low-interest loans for financing new and rehabbed housing, and resurgent efforts to rebuild the public school system. Federal funds, typically targeting low and moderate income persons and communities are now used to subsidize persons with incomes nearly 200 percent of the Chicago median family income.

In this historical context, community activist-researchers and applied policy advocates met to support work on common issues affecting the life quality and living conditions of most Chicagoans. It was also in this context that CWED was established: a coalition with a mission to help primarily low-income communities build viable economies through comprehensive community-directed economic development projects and activities while promoting public policies and social practices to facilitate those goals.

CWED activists also criticized Mayor Byrne's neighborhood planning board process: If this process was patterned after the extant citizen participation structure for allowing community input into the use and allocation of Community Development Block Grant (CDBG) funds, the mayor would coopt neighborhood-based initiatives by appointing nominees from the community who would favor the urban development policies of the Byrne administration. Moreover, under the proposed neighborhood planning board process, the City would be divided into eleven planning districts; the CBD would be kept separate. Under the plan, released during the summer before the 1983 mayoral election, no money was allocated for the operations of the planning boards, for neighborhood improvements, or for community development projects. CWED supporters attacked the proposal as politically motivated, believing that Mayor Byrne had no intention of implementing it in a viable way.

CWED activists had the active support of scholar-activists and social action researchers from universities and civic institutions on all of these issues. Their ability to work together was tested in struggles around significant policy issues in this period and thereafter.

Enter City Hall, Chicago Style

The collaboration that was formed in the early history of CWED was carried into the reform regimes of Mayor Harold Washington (1983-1987) and his successor, Eugene Sawyer (1987-1989). This influence took two forms.

First, the CWED Platform was based on in-depth analysis of Chicago's economic development conditions and on the experiences of community development practitioners and social action researchers. This platform provided the basis of Harold Washington's urban and community development policy. It manifested itself in the public policy pronouncement called Chicago Works Together, published in 1984. The authors contend that the central tenets in the CWED Platform, in the Washington transition papers, and in the Empowerment Zone are consistent—that the basic principles in the Empowerment Zone concept and in Chicago's own Empowerment Zone Strategic Plan are products from the work of those social action researchers who were instrumental in forming Mayor Washington's urban and community development policy and the ideas guiding the CWED Platform.

Second, CWED influenced the development of the Washington-Sawyer urban and community development policy because CWED founders and early members were recruited for critical staff and advisory positions in the Washington and Sawyer administrations. Four of the five founding members of CWED became instrumental officials in the major development departments of these administrations. Seven early members of CWED served in key advisory bodies as mayoral appointees. The authors of the CWED Platform were the principal drafters of the Washington papers and of Chicago Works Together.

Moreover, it is no accident that the CWED-UICUED connection in the history of the Empowerment Zone collaboration and struggles is so strong. A line of thought and intellectual descent leads directly from CWED and UICUED, through the Washington-Sawyer administrations, to the Empowerment Zone. The Empowerment Zone mobilization and the community's involvement in framing the Empowerment Zone policy and the local initiative originate in the connections between CWED and the Center for Urban Economic Development at the University of Illinois (UICUED).

Finally, the mobilization of the communities and neighborhood participants around the Empowerment Zone process in Chicago originated with CWED members, in affiliation with staff and faculty members associated with UICUED.

The Work of the Interim EZ/EC Coordinating Council

In October 1993, CWED staff was invited to meet with Vice-President Gore and his advisors to discuss the application process for Empowerment Zone designations. In these sessions, federal policy makers hoped to hear directly how communities intended to ensure that applicants were committed to bottom-up participation and collaboration rather than partnership for the sake of claiming another pot of public resources. Many of the recommendations that were made in these sessions were incorporated into the guidelines of the Empowerment Zone Program.

During this period, the *New York Times* published an article by Nicholas Lemann that questioned the success of the community development movement, beyond housing. The author raised serious doubts about the Empowerment Zone, calling it another failed Enterprise

Zone program. Against this background, CWED decided to use its December annual meeting, "Communities at the Crossroad," as an opportunity for dialogue about the future of community development. Participants would review the lessons and reports produced by academic institutions and community organizations.

The keynote speaker was Roy Priest, Director of Community Planning and Development for HUD, who later served as chair of the Federal Inter-Agency Task Force on Empowerment Zones. Priest challenged local government to listen to communities, accepting their representatives as equal partners. He challenged communities to take hold of their future. Shortly thereafter, CWED members resolved to inform and organize communities across the city to participate in the Empowerment Zone process.

By the time the Mayor of Chicago appointed the Interim Empowerment Zone/Enterprise Communities Coordinating Council (EZ/EC CC), the community outside government had begun to mobilize through the existing networks and community-based coalitions that already knew about the EZ process. Moreover, activists and support agents had developed a considerable body of ideas, principles, and innovative programs that could inform the formal selection process. In Chicago, in January 1994, the weekend of Martin Luther King's Birthday, CWED held a series of EZ informational meetings to brief members of the community development movement, practitioners in community economic development, elected and appointed public officials, administrators, and social action researchers on the official HUD regulations for the application process. About 125 persons attended.

At the meeting it was resolved that each community practitioner would return to his or her home community to mobilize the residents and the constituents of the appropriate organizations to apply for HUD designation as an Empowerment Zone or an Enterprise Community. This initial outreach work was done through community volunteers, service agencies, and civic activists without public or foundation funding.

Community activists also pledged that those who were based in community areas or neighborhoods ultimately designated would work to generate resources to build viable communities among eligible but unnominated census tracts. This was germane, because only 200,000 people and 20 square miles could be included in an Empowerment Zone application. (At least 1.25 million people, inhabiting nearly 80 square miles of residential census tracts, were eligible.) On that occasion, when CWED convened the meeting between community development organizations and invited government and legislative representatives to review the Empowerment Zone regulations, the elements of the Chicago EZ met for the first time. Over the next 18 months, scores of meetings and conferences were held throughout the city.

Additional support was offered by the academic administrators and applied researchers in attendance. They promised to work to build technical assistance support for communities and neighborhood constituents that sought to apply. This technical support would continue, once the nominated communities were identified and after prospective designation by the federal government.

On February 26, UICUED and CWED cosponsored a citywide technical assistance conference and a forum. Prospective applicants and academic and social action researchers provided input on the principles that would govern the boundary selection process. The selection criteria were drafted in a series of workshop sessions. The conference, which was funded by the Continental Bank (Bank of America), drew more than 200 people from all over the city. All segments of the public policy spectrum were represented: business, banking, government admini-strators, social scientists, legalists, social workers, culture workers, housing and community development practitioners, and activists, as well as ordinary grassroots citizen activists. This was the first formative meeting of the EZ partnership in Chicago.

After the conference, the UIC Great Cities program and the CWED staff convened a small work group that agreed to review the edited draft criteria, known as "area principles" (see below), and to prepare the forwarding documents to the city administration. The criteria to which the February conferees agreed were used to select the nominated communities and census tracts that ultimately would be submitted to HUD through the City of Chicago and the Governor of Illinois.

In early February 1994 the community hosted the Vice-President's Chicago visit to kick off the Empowerment Zone program. At that time, all Chicago was concerned about the "19 children on Keystone," who were left unattended by their parents. Several blocks away, however, at Lucy Flower High School, residents, youths, and other community stakeholders were explaining to the Vice-President how the Empowerment Zone could help ensure that children would not become "throwaway items" in the society. In late February, the City of Chicago hosted its first Empowerment Zone information session, following the conference at UIC held early that month.

The Seven Area Principles

These principles informed the selection criteria for nominating applicants for EZ designation:

1. The nomination applications should identify assets, both economic and institutional.
2. The resident/neighborhood applicants must demonstrate potential for building collaboration within and outside the targeted area.
3. The targeted area of the application must have an anchor organization with a record of service and accomplishment, and must

encourage the creation of new entities that can address the area's needs innovatively.

4. Show how the applicants will encourage leveraging of nonpublic funds with public funds to encourage utilization in addressing the aims of the local Strategic Plan.
5. Demonstrate how economic displacement will be addressed and how the area plan creates sustainable communities.
6. Demonstrate the capacity to plan, organize, and institute the goals and objectives of the plan.
7. Demonstrate how the community will be well served by public transportation.

The Selection Process and Sanctioning by City Council

In early March 1994, the mayor appointed an Interim Empowerment Zone/Enterprise Community-Coordinating Council. This 15-member group was charged with selecting the census tracts that were to be included in the HUD application from the city and from the State of Illinois as the nominating entity, and with naming the community-based agents of the selected community areas and census tracts. With the support of UICUED, the UIC Great Cities Program, the University of Chicago, and several consulting firms of legalists and urban designers, the Interim Coordinating Council designed and implemented a selection process; this process already had received substantial input from citizens, community groups, and research institutions. The Mayor's Office and the City Council members stayed relatively clear of the selection process, at least outwardly.

City Council members had a different relationship to the early EZ process. The most aggressive aldermen came from wards on the West Side; the most indifferent came from the South Side wards. The major point of contention was whether to include the South Side communities that lacked an industrial corridor with the East Side lake front communities north of 71st Street. The issue was how to assure the presence of "economic engines" in each designated area. This issue was resolved by including the Southwest Side industrial belt, which includes the historical stockyards (the Back of the Yards area, where Saul Alinsky first worked as an organizer in Chicago), as part of the South Side noncontiguous area of the Empowerment Zone. Thus, although none of the applicants on the South Side of Chicago included industrial corridors, one was included within the designated boundary because it represented one of the city's fastest-growing industrial areas.

Another major question was whether public housing should be included within all zone boundaries. Most members of the commission believed that if the proposed Empowerment Zone was to represent the truly unempowered, public housing residents should be at the top of the list. Inclusion of all public housing developments, however, would eliminate other persons in need. A compromise was reached: the City, as the nominating applicant for the Chicago EZ would request a waiver to treat all public housing residents as resident beneficiaries. This request was denied, however.

Thirty-three groups of communities submitted applications; portions of eleven ultimately were selected for nomination. Each applicant group had to submit a uniform application, outlining a strategic plan that embodied their vision of change, through comprehensive development, building partnerships to obtain internal as well as external resources, and by demonstrating sufficient capacity to carry out the vision and the Strategic Plan. (It is significant to note that these strategic plans, so important for determining inclusion in the EZ boundaries, have not been used to drive the awarding of EZ monies to carry them forward.)

In early April, after the submission deadline, the applicants had to present their strategic conception. Most groups made collaborative presentations suggesting that some previous linkage existed. Finally, after some more dispute about the boundaries, the selection map was presented to the mayor in mid-April. The mayor then introduced the map of city-designated community areas and census tracts to the City Council, and it was approved in May 1994.

After the Empowerment Zone map was submitted to the City Council, the next task of the Interim Coordinating Council was the designation of Enterprise Communities (ECs). The committee decided to name three such communities.

The EZ is distinguished from the ECs in the following ways:

♦ The EZ communities share in $100 million; the ECs do not.
♦ The ECs are required to designate an anchoring community agency for administering EC activities, which (if that EC was chosen) would receive up to $3 million for operations and coordinating programs.
♦ The designated ECs receive bonus points on federal applications for other federal funds for which residents and local businesses are eligible.
♦ ECs are eligible to share in EDI funds as if they were designated as an EZ.

The selected Empowerment Zone in Chicago was noncontiguous; it contained slightly under 200,000 persons and covered slightly less than 19 square miles. With the inclusion of the ECs in the policy process, if not in the money, the Chicago Empowerment Zone/Enterprising Community process would have a direct and indirect effect on 400,000 persons, and perhaps on another 150,000 who worked in the proposed Zone but did not live there.

This stage of the early planning process had been marked by massive mobilization of ordinary community residents and the leading role of community-based organizations. Their leadership would carry over into the strategic planning phase of the process during late April through June 1994.

Promises of Technical Assistance to the Community Areas

As early as the first EZ briefing session, representatives of the research and policy development community made commitments to the participants in the Empowerment Zone/Enterprising Community process to offer various forms of technical assistance (TA). Numerous examples of technical support and assistance have been documented, but ongoing assistance generally lagged behind the promises.

Among the TA providers other than CWED, the most active supporters of the Empowerment Zone in Chicago were the Urban Land Institute (ULI), the Chicago Jobs Council (CJC), and the Chicago Initiative (TCI). Other agencies also were active, such as the Center for Neighborhood Technology (CNT), UIC's Center for Urban Economic Development, the Neighborhood Capital Budget Group (NCBG), and the Neighborhood Institute (TNI). Still other TA agencies have supported the EZ/ECs in an adjunctive role and by promoting one or more of the concepts in the Four HUD principles discussed above. Moreover, the excitement and interest in the national EZ initiative and in Chicago's prospects for designation apparently promoted discussion and consciousness about the principles underlying community development work. This has been the case in the major educational and research institutions in Chicago and among foundations and donors.

The UIC Center for Urban Economic Development, the North-western University Center for Urban Affairs and Policy Research, and Loyola and DePaul Universities had conducted applied research in community development before the EZ concept. Now, other institutions also became active in community research and applied community development, including Roosevelt University, the University of Chicago, Chicago State University, Illinois Institute of Technology, and Spertus and Columbia Colleges.

PRAG has encouraged involvement by many research centers in collaborative and social action research. Perhaps it is not coincidental that the growth of PRAG has been paralleled by the establishment of new community development and urban policy institutes in the Chicago area, hosted by educational and research institutions at DePaul University (The Eagan Center), at Spertus College, at Loyola University, and at Chicago State University. The Great Cities Initiative at UIC has supplied leadership to an urban research consortium to provide technical and support assistance to the communities in and near Chicago's Empowerment Zone. The consortium has involved UIC, Chicago State University, Roosevelt, DePaul, and Loyola Universities, IIT, the University of Chicago, and Northwestern University. All of these initiatives wish to combine their efforts to address the questions of reducing or eradicating poverty through various related approaches to community development.

Some of the initiatives by technical assistance providers have not extended throughout the Zone. We have observed a disproportionate concentration of technical assistance and support services on the Near West, Near Northwest, and West Sides of the Chicago EZ, perhaps because UIC and its Great Cities work have been concentrated in Pilsen, Little Village, and the West Side Lawndale communities. Perhaps this is focus is appropriate, but it creates an access problem for the overall Chicago EZ process. In short, technical support to the EZ process has been uneven and irregular. This has impacted the level and quality of community participation in the EZ process.

Getting the Word Out to the 'Hoods

The Empowerment Zone participants, who convened the community involvement activities, have had to endeavor under constraints of increasing demands placed upon meager outreach resources. The managers of the formal process provided no assistance and no support for aggressive mobilization of residents inside the "Zone," a reference to the overall Empowerment Zone process in Chicago. Few foundations made funding available for the Empowerment Zone outreach, to Empowerment Zone volunteer organizers and facilitators, or to the local community cluster operations. The active core of the EZ process was the "clusters"; the collaborating anchor groups within the major regions of the Chicago EZ.

The city was slow to provide educational materials indicating a broad partnership across the EZ communities. Moreover, the City did not support initiatives undertaken by the local Zone community clusters and their organizers as they attempted to build open meetings, hold conferences and informational educational forums for citizens and businesses in the Zone. The City provided technical staff assistance to the fledgling community organizations for only a brief period after the submittal to HUD. This occurred between August and early December 1994. At that time the City promoted the notion of developing some "fast-track projects" that could be brought on-line quickly to demonstrate to HUD, should HUD visit, that Chicago's Empowerment Zone was ready to proceed, if it were designated. In short, after the submission to HUD, the Empowerment Zone Clusters were left largely to their own devices by all but a few institutions. After designation in late December, the City abandoned them altogether.

The Citywide Strategic Planning Process
and the Chicago Strategic Plan

Between the end of April and the end of June 1994, the City managed the strategic planning process. This process was opened up to shared participation through the aggressive efforts of community leaders across the city. In particular, leaders drawn from the EZ/EC cluster organizations played major roles. The city planners who managed the process, under community pressure, altered their preconceived approach to the development of a standard Strategic Plan. This allowed for the infusion of progressive, creative, innovative ideas from community and human development practitioners into the EZ strategic planning process. Ordinary citizens, who had witnessed the failure of "business and politics as usual" intervention in public policy, made proposals to ensure accountability in the EZ implementation process.

Social action researchers and policy analysts presented information on the best practices in urban community and human development, economics, and social policy implementation, accumulated over the past 30 years. Business interests, community groups, and government agents did reach agreement about the strategic goals, the program objectives, and the basic approach to accomplishing the intent of the four HUD principles and the seven area principles. There was no consensus on sharing power or resources once designation was awarded.

The Mayor and the Governor signed a progressive Strategic Plan that was intended to guide the implementation, monitoring, and evaluation of accomplishments of the Chicago EZ/EC process. The representatives of community cluster organizations approved the Chicago EZ Strategic Plan. They believed that their conception of the governance process, as proposed in the HUD application and certified by the Mayor and the Governor, was consistent with Congressional intent and with the HUD regulations governing the EZ initiative. (The Mayor and the City Council differed substantially. Their actions since HUD designation have confirmed EZ/EC residents' and community activists' fears that "business and politics as usual" would prevail in the implementation of the Chicago EZ. This divergence of views on the substance of the EZ policy and the role of community-based groups in the EZ/EC has been at the heart of the debate within the EZ partnership in Chicago.)

The Chicago Empowerment Zone strategic planning process has been defined as one of the most inclusive citizen participation processes of policy development in the city's history. Between April 24, 1994 and June 27, 1994 a series of citywide strategic planning sessions, writing sessions, and negotiation sessions were held, involving the city planning officials, the representatives of the various community clusters, paid professional consultants, and interested business persons and citizens. A few aldermen and/or their representatives attended some of these sessions. For the most part, however, the community had to rely on its members' energies, creative talents, and expertise to leave its imprint on the Chicago Empowerment Zone Strategic Plan.

Moreover, the City paid the private development specialists substantial amounts of money to design and produce a competitive application for submission to HUD. The community clusters did not have the benefit of paid consultants. They were forced to rely on the facilitative services of the CWED staff, some university researchers, and volunteer professionals who lived and/or worked in the communities constituting the Chicago Empowerment Zone/Enterprising Communities. The communities had no battery of institutional researchers and program developers; nor did they have clerical workers to process the proposals and counter proposals as the Strategic Plan proceeded through various drafts over a seven-week period.

Content of the Chicago EZ Strategic Plan

The Chicago Empowerment Zone application consisted of a one-volume Strategic Plan, three supporting volumes of documents and three additional volumes, each representing one of the nominated Enterprise Communities. The Chicago Empowerment Zone planning process differed from the process for the developing Chicago Enterprise Communities. However, while the applications for the EZ and the ECs had to be submitted separately, the Chicago EZ process includes the Empowerment Zone plus the three nominated Enterprise Community areas. All of the documents were submitted to HUD as a part of one process governed by the same goals and themes, but HUD considered the EZ and the EC applications separately. Although the ECs remain a part of the EZ process in Chicago, they were not funded by HUD.

The Chicago EZ Strategic Plan has two principal goals: to alleviate poverty and to reinvent government by altering the relationships between citizens and the government authorities so as to create mutual accountability and mutual participation in decision making. The Strategic Plan is based on the four HUD principles and on a series of interlocking basic principles that participants in the Chicago Empowerment Zone process have agreed to uphold throughout the process. In addition to the goals statement and the principles, the Plan contains a series of integrated, programmatic objectives called the Seven Strategic Initiatives. All three of these elements—the goals, the principles, and the Seven Initiatives—were crafted by community representatives and supported by city staff members. The overall service delivery and support program in the Strategic Plan, seen as a comprehensive, interrelated system, can be accessed through any of the seven initiative areas by Zone residents as individuals, as families, or as entire communities.

agencies

proceed

Goals and Strategic Objectives

The strategic goals of the Chicago EZ Strategic Plan are to reduce poverty at the individual, family, peer, and community level and to reinvent government by empowering EZ residents, as service recipients, to hold public and private service providers accountable for the services they provide. Thus, this approach might alter the relationship between the governors and the governed. In support of these strategic goals, some twenty "overarching" principles were included to guide the implementation, monitoring, and assessment of outcomes expected from the EZ Strategic Plan.

The substantive program of the Strategic Plan is organized (as stated above) around seven strategic initiatives or integrated program areas, through which zone projects are to be facilitated:

- Economic opportunity/economic development;
- Affordable housing;
- Human and organizational development;
- Health and human services;
- Youth futures;
- Public/community safety; and
- Cultural diversity.

In addition to these aspects of the Plan, there was the community proposal on governance of the Chicago EZ process. After 18 months of the process, and nine months after designation, this issue still had not been resolved. However, by May 1995, the City was able to pass through City Council a governance ordinance that negated the strong role of the EZ/EC community clusters and discount the notion of shared power expressed in the EZ strategic plan.

In the period after Chicago was designated as an Empowerment Zone, the attitude of city officials seemed to be the local cluster organizations would "just go away" or disintegrate. They have not dissipated, however, despite obstacles to their maintenance.

Whither the EZ Process?

After the applications were submitted to HUD, the city administration focused most of its outreach resources on corporate business, primarily the banking community. This was not wrong, but it neglected the broad mobilization of the residents in the Zone. The Chicago banking community agreed to commit some $2.5 billion to reinvestment in Chicago communities, including more than $1 billion for targeted reinvestment in the Empowerment Zone community areas.

On the surface, this commitment by lending institutions seems progressive. Some critics, however, believe that unregulated physical redevelopment of Chicago's poorest, most distressed neighborhoods may accelerate economic displacement and gentrification in the EZ communities. Empowerment Zone community activists have asserted that the best way to avert this outcome is to ensure that community residents and their representatives are full partners, with equity in the implementation, monitoring, and assessment of the Empowerment Zone process as well as in the initial planning.

Certainly the community was progressively involved in the strategic planning of the Chicago Empowerment Zone process, especially before HUD submission and the designation of Chicago as an Empowerment Zone.

One could argue that, after the excitement surrounding the initial mobilization for Chicago's participation in the national Empowerment Zone competition, much of the not-for-profit research and policy community reduced its participation or lost interest in helping communities prepare for implementation. Some commentators suggested that the overall planning process had been chaotic and confusing. Others thought the process would not lead to designation as an Empowerment Zone. Still others thought the process was too latent with politics. The authors contend that the democratic process is political. It is often messy and chaotic, especially as it relates to the demand for shared power between public officials who possess power and distressed social agents who do not.

Although many agents of colleges and universities understood the need for mass outreach, most were overwhelmed by the attempt to sustain involvement by thousands of potential Zone resident activists. The major educational and research institutions in Chicago responded only partially and unevenly even to the demand of Empowerment Zone-based community organizations to establish computerized networks. Some Empowerment Zone-based groups were able to go on line, but the great majority were not.

The main forms of CBO linkages within the Zone remained the traditional ones, although local community clusters have established new connections with groups, institutions, and associations both outside and inside the Zone. Groups with a tradition of grassroots organizing and with some outreach capacity were able to bring the constituent base of the Empowerment Zone's clusters into the process. Thus, the difficulties in maintaining constituents' participation in Zone activities and processes were often related to Zone facilitators' ability to tap resources. In one region, the most aggressively active sectors were the ward organizations. In another, the local business organizations and chambers of commerce were more active. Therefore, this involvement tended to reflect the orientation of the regional and subregional clusters that emerged during the Empowerment Zone process. In other regions and subregions, ward politicians and business groups were less strongly involved, for various reasons. In these communities, the Zone activist had to rely principally on the churches and/or the traditional forms of community organization to anchor the building process. Few external resources have been put at the disposal of the cluster collaborations.

Thus, the resources available to organizers varied across the Zone. Moreover, cluster and subcluster organizations had varying amounts of resources available to sustain the local anchoring organizations through the two years of the EZ process. Over this period, all but the most committed and most conscientious have wavered. They were taxed by the brutally long Empowerment Zone developmental processes. The young are adventurous and impatient, with short attention spans. The elderly are committed, but within the range of their limitations. The adults of productive age are distressed and are starved for resources. They all have experienced crises that might seem small and easily resolved in middle-class and affluent families and communities. Not so among the poor, who have limited discretionary resources. Yet, thus far, the clusters have survived.

In the Zone, there has been a constant, taxing struggle to sustain participation among local residents who have been recruited into the process. Many of these individuals are easily frustrated; still others are readily distracted. Thus, a major internal battle has been waged to keep the participants collectively focused on the goals of the process and to prevent individuals from becoming involved in distractions that tend to take their toll during protracted struggles.

Strategic Planning in the 'Hoods: Three Models

As noted above, the various clusters took different paths to nomination as participating entities. In one case, the politicians in the community areas met and framed a strategic plan for the area based on the political leaders' degree of influence. A cluster also formed around the region's business community, supported by heads of community service agencies and university researchers who were familiar with the community development needs of the region or cluster area. Moreover, this cluster, as it emerged, received some support from prominent city and state political leaders in building alliances and in forming connections.

In another region, the evolving cluster had little help from the politicians connected to City Hall. On the contrary, some of the area's political leaders were hostile toward the initiative because it required too much citizen participation, Another set of politicians distanced themselves from the process because they viewed the cluster leaders as either too independent or too adversarial toward the regular political agents. The cluster leaders were opposed to the development policies pursued by the aldermen, both inside and outside City Council. This cluster essentially was organized around the community-based development and social service organizations within the Zone communities of the region. The strength of the outreach and the residents' level of involvement stemmed from the CBOs' capacity to mobilize resources for development of the EZ process at local, regional, and Zone-wide levels.

In a third cluster, the leadership was deeply rooted in the organizational and political life of the local institutions, which were the basis of the cluster's planning. Involvement by ordinary citizen-residents was limited, a problematic situation. Involvement also was limited to constituents' participation within the orbit of single local institutions. Moreover, this mode of outreach is parochial: It limits participants' diversity and restricts the capacity to mobilize resources from parts of the community outside these institutions.

These scenarios reveal several distinct models for the development of the strategic planning that governed the emergent clusters' application process. In all but one of the scenarios, citizens' broad participation in the planning process was limited, save through institutionalized structures that virtually predetermined the flow of influence and controlled the process from the top down. These scenarios demonstrated various ways of producing community plans for change and development. In each model, the key is the cluster organization's collective capacity to mobilize resources to sustain residents' focused participation at all levels of the process. Each cluster may have the potential for sustained community and citizen participation; it remains to be seen whether they will realize that potential. This has been particularly tenuous, when there is a climate that is indifferent to, if not hostile to the development of clusters as viable centers of the local EZ process.

On Sustaining Citizen Participation and Collaborative Activity: Key Lessons from the EZ Experience

We speak about collaborative citizen participation in relative rather than absolute terms. That is, on any set of policy questions, all of the clusters might resist the centralized public policy making that typically characterizes city government in Chicago. Certain conditions must prevail, however, to generate a sustained collective commitment to community empowerment politics and the extension of democratic practices.

First, the anchor group must have access to the resources to initiate, maintain outreach and sustain contact with community residents. Without these resources, the anchor organization will resort to mobilizing tactics that rely on the constituent networks closest to itself. Such involvement may be intense, but it will not be diverse or extensive. The social costs will be limited participation by broad sections of the community and a lack of desired diversity.

Second, we believe that the independence of the local community clusters is threatened by the undue influence of the traditional political leaders and by the pervasive tendency to withhold information and to control the policy process. Politicians and government policy makers tend to restrict access to power in decision making. They are reluctant to share power in implementation, oversight, and assessment for fear that the public will hold them accountable and that citizens will gain access to what most politicians consider privileged knowledge. This is precisely what the Empowerment Zone is designed to overcome.

In the Chicago EZ process, the community collaborative partnership has been the most vibrant and most progressive aspect of the planning phase. Chicago had the most open and most forward-looking planning process of the nationally designated cities. The establishment of a permanent governance process, however, has been one of the most regressive from the standpoint of sharing power and respecting the community aspect of the partnership. Citizens must be assured of participation in the formal policy decisions about where money will be spent and how the EZ Title XX funds will be used. Moreover, the city's political leaders do not want to be held accountable to comply with the EZ goals statement and the central initiatives.

Furthermore, as we have stated, if a commitment to community-directed development is to be sustained in community planning and development policy, then democratic characteristics and practices must be present.

Third, the cluster leaders generally did very well in involving the broader community in developing the initial cluster or community-area planning groups. The resulting plans, taken together, reflect the best practices in community (and community economic) development. This general finding is not surprising because most of the leading figures in the Chicago Empowerment Zone process have a history of participation in community associations, networks, and coalitions where these ideas prevail. It is not surprising that this community leadership had surfaced within the Empowerment Zone process to drive the mobilization and planning phase.

Fourth, we observed that the clusters had access to highly skilled researchers, policy analysts, and program developers from within their own ranks or that their leaders had access to such resources at universities and research institutions, or from among the providers of community-oriented technical assistance. Generally, those groups of applicants which lacked these mobilizable resources were not selected. This should not imply, however, that political connections were not a factor in selecting the nominated groups.

The analysis suggests that (as in most situations) the Empowerment Zone nominees' selection process was not a level playing field on which constituents across the city were equally eligible to be selected. Nevertheless, the group-sanctioned selection criteria ensured that the best-qualified applicants could be selected. We assert that politics played a part, despite the relative fairness of the process. For one thing, not all of the community areas that applied had equal access to the resources required to assure selection. The cluster areas that were selected could mobilize greater social, technical, and organizational resources than those which were not. They were also better able to mobilize political resources within the rules. This is not an indictment of the process but a statement of apparent fact.

Fifth, did those who were selected deserve selection? In our assessment, all of the successful applicants had merit; that is, they met the selection criteria. It is also true, however, that some applicants who were not accepted were equally meritorious. On what basis were the choices made? From our vantage point, the unsuccessful applicants could not mobilize sufficient sociopolitical resources to bring to bear on their selection, in contrast to the successful candidates.

The analysis suggests that several related factors were related to success or lack of success. The first factor is the degree and quality of technical resources that the groups of applicants were able to mobilize. The second is a set of sociopolitical factors: The more social networks the applicant groups could draw upon and the more political resources they could bring to bear on the process, the greater their chances of selection. One such factor was the degree of perceived ability to mobilize constituents; another was the degree of integration into existing networks.

Post-Selection Activity

One of the first tasks of the local community entities that were nominated by the EZ/EC Coordinating Council was to continue developing the local organization of participants in the Empowerment Zone process at the community level. These local community units, or clusters, vary across the local community Zone process, which includes the EZs as well as the ECs.

Clusters also vary as to the quantity and quality of residents' involvement. In some clusters, youth have played an active role. In fact, they were responsible for inclusion of the Youth Futures initiative in the strategic plan. In other clusters, the leadership is held by ward organization members; again, in at least one cluster, the local businesses in association have taken the leading role.

Participation by institutional activists and leaders—the church, universities, political organizations, and labor organizations—also varies. Involvement by public housing residents has ranged from nonexistent to nominal. The regularity of meetings varies as well; some clusters met weekly, and others met less than once a month. Finally, some of the clusters have formal bylaws, a few have become chartered under state law, and at least one has filed for an IRS tax exemption status. Some clusters have become or have remained organized into subregional, local community-area clusters, with committees and task forces; they mirror the internal organization of the regional Empowerment Zone cluster.

Social researchers, planners, and policy analysts within the community clusters have been involved to varying degrees. The University of Illinois at Chicago, through its Great Cities program and UICUED, has offered the most sustained participation among the educational institutions. UIC, however, has been criticized, perhaps unjustifiably, because it has concentrated its interaction and support among community groups in the Pilsen-Little Village and Near West Side communities, next to the campus.

What is true of UIC is generally true of most research and technical assistance agencies, centers of higher learning, and corporate consultants: These entities have tended to concentrate their involvement and services on the Pilsen-Little Village and the Near West Side of the Empowerment Zone in Chicago. The one major exception has been CWED. Other development coalitions, such as the Chicago Rehab Network and the Neighborhood Capital Budget Group, have continued to do related work, CWED has focused on facilitating community empowerment, within and alongside the EZ initiative.

Community involvement across the EZ has varied, depending upon the resources available to local clusters. Citizen participation and "bottom-up" processes do not simply occur; like anything else, they must be built. Some observers in both private and public sectors would have us believe that community development organizations involved in the EZ process are not bottom-up. These organizations, however, are important elements of a community and must be viewed as critical institutions that are connected to people.

In addition, residents are not monolithic. If we keep in mind that we hold elections in which less than 35 percent of the voting population participates, we must also have realistic expectations about involvement in the Empowerment Zone. Residents in these communities have been disappointed time after time. Most of those who became involved, first were already involved in some aspect of volunteerism and civic participation. For many others, it was their first opportunity to meet and work collaboratively with others who are committed to rebuilding some aspect of their communities. Participation will likely increase among local residents when they can see and work at activities that improve their material circumstances and their quality of life.

Key Issues of the Continuing Empowerment Zone Struggle: A Concluding Note

As exhaustive as the Empowerment Zone process has been for the most active participants, the process may have benefits far beyond the award of $100 million, which may attract billions of dollars of new investments in Empowerment Zone communities. The Empowerment Zone experiment also may be a catalyst to regenerate moribund local economies, improve housing, and upgrade the physical infrastructure in residential as well as commercial and industrial developments. Empowerment Zone implementation may well increase the numbers of people who live in the Zone, who gain access to meaningful employment, and who enhance their occupational skills; and individual, family, and collective accumulation of assets will likely be the result. The Chicago Empowerment Zone certainly has stimulated creative ways to address numerous socioeconomic and cultural problems, which contribute to nonviable social relations in some of the most distressed neighborhoods in the city.

Moreover, the Empowerment Zone experience may well create windows of opportunity by mobilizing internal resources among Zone residents and their organizations and institutions. The mobilization of Empowerment Zone residents also may awaken the poor and distressed throughout the city, who receive the Empowerment Zone's message of hope: If it can be done in the Zone, then possibly more concerted efforts can be devised to respond to the needs of non-Zone residents. Perhaps the principles that form the cornerstone of the national Empowerment Zone demonstration initiative can be extended, through collective action and enlightened public policy making, to other arenas of government and their allocation practices. A clear hope is that the poor, inside and outside the Zone, will press for municipal service distribution reform proportionate to their tax contributions to the city budget.

The opportunities for Empowerment Zone residents, business owners, and organization leaders to participate in planning might be extended to other areas of public life and other areas of public policy development. This point applies to the continuing EZ process as well as to the overall structures of urban governance. It includes substantive issues such as education, health and safety (including crime reduction), transportation, and capital development. Currently, the prevailing thought is that poor people do not pay a fair share of local taxes. Current research suggests that they do not reap benefits from the taxes they pay.

These are aspects of a progressive strategic vision of the Empowerment Zone developmental process, as well as the extension of that process to urban governance and policy development. Before we can realize this vision, however, some issues in the current Empowerment Zone process must be resolved.

The Critical Issue of Governance

Key it but why?

The most disheartening aspect of the governance issue in Chicago is that it began with the most deeply involved and most inclusive community-based process. In the end, however, Chicago remains the only designated EZ city that has failed to acknowledge community structures, such as the clusters, in the formal makeup of the Empowerment Zone governance. It is important to include individuals from the community among the overseers, but the value of collaboration, self-determination, and community self-sufficiency demands the existence of structures in the community to be responsible for positive change.

The greatest drama in the current stage of the Chicago Empowerment Zone process has concerned the level and extent of community inclusion in the ongoing governance of the Zone: the level and proportion of community-selected representatives in the permanent governance body, the management, allocation and distribution of Empowerment Zone funds, and the degree of autonomy of the clusters of the participating entities, relative to the other partners in the Empowerment Zone process. The character of the Empowerment Zone partnership has yet to be determined. At this time it is not clear that the city officials are willing to accept the implications of building a meaningful partnership between government and business, with effective community participation.

Chicago city officials are reluctant to accept the concept of shared public power. This concept, in the context of the Empowerment Zone, suggests that the community representatives, like the business representatives in the process, have equity. Equity is what the communities are seeking: They wish to be recognized as full partners in making decisions about substantive issues as well as process issues, but the city has not been willing to extend its concept of partnership building beyond procedural matters. The fiercest battles have not been about fashioning a vision of change, but about implementing that vision into the practice of governance and into decisions about resource allocation.

A classic example concerns the city ordinance establishing a permanent governance body. The mayor resisted the communities' efforts to create a body that would have more than advisory status with respect to City Hall executives and the City Council. The ordinance, which was passed by the City Council in late May 1995, did not even recognize a role for the Empowerment Zone clusters at any level of formal decision making. Furthermore, the ordinance gave the mayor the power to appoint 37 of the 39 members of the advisory body. It reserved to city administrators the power to hire staff members to the governance body, and it made City Council the ultimate body for determining resource allocation. This is hardly "reinventing government"; it virtually assures the continuation of "business (and politics) as usual" in Chicago public policy formation.

Most critics and community activists were not surprised that the current mayoral regime took this position. Community participants in the Empowerment Zone process were more disappointed in the ward aldermen, especially those representing wards in the Empowerment Zone area, for their almost reactionary rejection of the Empowerment Zone principles and for siding with the mayor against their constituents and representatives of agencies working to empower Zone residents.

Perhaps the greatest source of disappointment was the virtual silence from community empowerment supporters in the foundations and the social policy and action research community; they remained mute while the principles asserted in Chicago for nearly two decades were trampled without a word of protest. HUD has expected the partners to the initial Strategic Plan to honor their claims and commitments, as stated in the application submitted in June 1994.

a long time

key points

The governance issue held up the development of the EZ/EC process for a considerable period between designation (December 1994) until it was settled (June 1996). Since then, the bureaucratic process processing service contracts has kept money from "hitting the streets." The governance impasse delivered a message: community activists should be wary of building partnerships with government and business entities: The community must have the resources to sustain the mobilization of disadvantaged residents and their organizations to sustain demands for inclusion. Hard work and good ideas are necessary but not sufficient to gain and retain a share of decision-making power. There is need for an informed, well-organized constituency, for it is unrealistic to expect that power wielders will give up power unless they are compelled to do so.

Moreover, the City must show a commitment to keep business as usual politics from demobilizing the activity and enthusiasm of EZ participants.

Furthermore, the collaborative relations between social action researchers and community activists were manifested in the recent Empowerment Zone process in Chicago. They reflect strengths as well as weaknesses. The great strengths were the networks and linkages that collaborative researchers and activists on the campus and in the community had built and nurtured. The weakness is the fact that these linkages tend not to be politically progressive enough to be useful to disadvantaged communities in their struggles to share power in making and implementing policy. When communities endorse the progressive ideas of the activist researchers in the academy and in applied research institutions, they do not appear to generate enough support from the social action researchers to effect political and public policy change. In the struggle surrounding the Empowerment Zone in Chicago, the constituents in the targeted communities found few allies who would speak out supporting the principles espoused by these so-called progressives.

Our conclusions are quite tentative, but they revolve around the themes we have outlined above. Collaborative research and policy action are essential to community building, and link empowerment objectives to developmental goals. The participants in these networks have made vital contributions to the development of strong networks and associations, linking activist researchers and policy analysts to organized communities in struggles for development, empowerment, and survival. In Chicago this network was important to the establishment of progressive public policy agendas and contributed to the rise to power of a progressive mayoral regime during the 1980s.

The development of collaborative networks, however, linking researchers to distressed communities and their key actors, is not sufficient. If these communities are to effect change in public policy, they require material resources to reach out, to educate, to organize, and to mobilize their constituents. They also need effective, committed, forward-looking leaders who are accountable to their constituents.

Finally, these communities require a political as well as a public policy strategy. In the Empowerment Zone process in Chicago, the activist communities had a vision of policy change, but they lacked consensus on a political strategy to guide their relations with friends and adversaries.

Endnotes

1. Process consists of activities and interactions between and among sanctioned decision makers as well as under represented individuals who unite to press demands on policy makers, operating within predetermined, agreed-upon rules. The EZ process consists of several aspects: planning, implementation, monitoring, and assessment. Here we are concerned with the first two of these dimensions, although we can suggest certain

implications for the remaining phases.

2. Wanda White uses the term _windows of opportunity_ to suggest that the Empowerment Zone process creates openings in the policy-making structures of government, whereby social activists can initiate reforms that improve ordinary citizens' quality of life and living standards through collective action.

3. The term _community activists_ typically denotes persons who, by profession or avocation, promote the work of organizations of people who are conscious of their identity of interest, condition, or location. In this case we broaden the concept to include nonprofessional, indigenous residents and other members of constituency-based communities.

4. For a model work using the social action research model, see Nyden and Wiewel (1991). Another relevant 'work on the Chicago context is Clavel and Wiewel (1991).

5. The National Economic Development and Law Center, the National Council on Community Economic Development, the Poverty and Race Research Action Council (PRRAC), and the National Low Income Housing Coalition are examples of national associations with links to local practitioners and Community Economic Development (CED) organizations and to networks of community service agencies across the country. These include policy advocacy networks as well as welfare reform and welfare rights organizations. The Leadership Development Network is cited among these proactive groups with national connections as well as connections to local civic and community activists. Other organizations exist as well, but we mention these for their past and present influence on the development of the Empowerment Zone process and on the articulation of the underlying ideas. Also see Ferman (1996) and Clavel and Wiewel (1991).

6. For more information on the distinctions between these policy initiatives, see President's Community Empowerment Board (1995); U.S. Department of Housing and Urban Development (1994-1995).

7. A number of researchers are studying the development of the local and national Empowerment Zone process, but few of the studies are ready for citation. However, Michael Bennett, Cedric Herring, and Doug Gills have initiated a national three-year study, funded in part by the UIC Great Cities Initiative, the MacArthur Foundation, and The Joyce Foundation. A clearinghouse has been established.

8. See publications of the Community Workshop on Economic Development; to obtain these publications, write to the organization at 100 South Morgan Street, Chicago, IL 60607.

9. See publications by the Community Workshop on Economic Development. Also see Community Renewal Society (1993); Kretzmann and McKnight (1993); and United Way of Chicago (1992, 1993, 1994).

10. By *modern* we refer to the confluence of developments and factors during the 1960s that gave rise to new forms of community organization. These originated in the urban movements, principally among African American people in the central cities, and were organized outside institutionalized politics. In Chicago, these organizations were distinct from the earlier neighborhood improvement associations, the citizens' associations, the labor and industrial-related organizations and the social institution-based groups identified with Saul Alinsky, and the still earlier benevolent societies and immigrant settlement housing support organizations of the late nineteenth and early twentieth centuries.

11. See Doug Gills (1991) and Alkalimat (1989). Also see Brechor and Costello (1991).

12. For various perspectives, see Clavel and Wiewel (1991). CBO

development under Mayor Washington are discussed in Gills (1991) and Alkalimat and Gills (1989); Also see Wiewel and Gills.

13. See Ferman op. cit.

14. See UICUED (1996).

15. See Squires, Bennett, Nyden and McCourt (1987).

16. Interview with Lou Krienberg, July 3, 1994.

Chapter 3

A Tale of Two Cities?

Profiles of Chicago's Empowerment Zone Residents and Non-Zone Residents

Cedric Herring

O ne of the goals of the Federal Empowerment Zone program is to rebuild communities in America's poverty-stricken inner cities. This policy is designed to empower people and communities in developing and implementing strategies to create job opportunities and sustainable community development. The legislation, however, contains some rather contradictory elements. For example, to qualify for designation as an urban Empowerment Zone (EZ), an area had to display pervasive poverty, high unemployment, and general social distress. These characteristics typically are associated with social isolation, alienation, political disenfranchisement, and inactivity in the public arena. Yet communities that were designated as Empowerment Zones were expected to involve ordinary citizens in the policy-making process through extraordinary levels of grassroots activism.

How do residents of Chicago's Empowerment Zone compare with residents from other Chicago-area communities in regard to social, political, and economic dispositions and activities? Most people understand that where a person lives makes a difference. We know that some neighborhoods have high poverty rates, while other communities appear to be centers of economic development and growth. Some communities have higher than usual crime rates. Still others are centers of political mobilization and activism. Yet it is difficult to know whether any of these generalizations accurately describe Chicago's Empowerment Zone.

It is not clear how residents of the Empowerment Zone compare with others from impoverished areas in Chicago, nor is it apparent how EZ residents compare with others in the metropolitan region. It is even more uncertain whether the characteristics of any of these communities, in themselves, have any effect on the residents' activities, lifestyles, or life chances.

In this chapter we attempt to determine not only the degree to which EZ communities differ from other communities in the Chicago metropolitan area, but also how EZ residents differ socially, politically, and economically from others in Chicagoland. We compare people who live in communities that were designated as part of Chicago's Empowerment Zone with (1) residents of other low-income communities in Chicago that applied unsuccessfully for designation as Enterprise Communities, (2) Chicago residents who live neither in the Empowerment Zone nor in any of the communities that applied to become Enterprise Communities, and (3) others who live in the Chicago metropolitan area but not in Chicago proper.

Community Characteristics and Political Involvement

Because Chicago's inner-city communities have become more heavily populated by blacks and other people of color, some analysts have stated that departing whites are taking with them the city's industrial base, the high-wage jobs, the tax base, and other elements that make it possible to provide quality education and necessary municipal services (e.g., Massey and Denton 1993). Others, however, believe that as African Americans and other people of color have become more prevalent in the central city, they have grown more able to empower themselves by electing their co-ethnics to city councils and school boards, and as mayors of major cities (e.g., Bobo and Gilliam 1990).

Black political empowerment, for example, is correlated with outcomes such as reductions in blacks' neonatal mortality rates (LaVeist 1992), lower rates and levels of political alienation among blacks (Bobo and Gilliam 1990), and increases in minority employment in administrative, professional, and protective jobs in cities (Dye and Renick 1981; Eisinger 1982). Even so, it is questionable whether population concentrations of African Americans provide political consolidation and empowerment or whether patterns of racial concentration and segregation might be regarded more accurately as apartheid.

Some critics of black empowerment strategies that rely on high levels of racial segregation suggest that inner cities represent concentrations of poverty, not of power. Massey and Denton (1993), for example, believe that segregation is not empowering, and describe several harmful effects of segregation. One of the most severe is the loss of civic and commercial services to the segregated neighborhood in the form of declining retail demand, increasing residential abandonment, business disinvestment, deindustrialization, and massive job loss. Furthermore, such "segregation also concentrates conditions such as drug use, joblessness, welfare dependency, teenage childbearing, and unwed parenthood, producing a social context where these conditions are not only common but the norm" (Massey and Denton 1993:13). In short, it concentrates self-destructive behavior in ways that are likely to offset any empowering effects of black neighborhoods.

Massey and Denton agree that segregation offers the *appearance* of political power in virtually all-black districts because such districts provide supermajorities and guarantee that African Americans can elect their own to office. They argue that while "the existence of solid black electoral districts...[does] create the potential for bloc voting along racial lines" (1993:155-56), it does not translate into the delivery of city services or even into patronage jobs. Rather, they say, racial segregation and isolation translate into the loss of opportunity to participate in effective coalition building with other groups, and into the subsequent loss of city services. Consequently many of these African American officials find it difficult to establish legislative coalitions with their non-black colleagues. Even worse, these representatives from hyper-segregated districts have little incentive to dilute their political base by encouraging any changes that would reduce levels of segregation. Thus, racial segregation makes it easier for white leaders to disregard and disinvest in African American communities.

Marable (1985, 1986) also suggests that racial segregation can lead to the political marginalization and insignificance of African Americans. He describes the mere concept of a "black politician" as essentially absurd, and reasons that the political system in America was designed to exclude representation by blacks. Thus, he argues, black politicians are often locked into a world of meaningless symbols that reinforce the ability of the white ruling class to rule. Marable believes that black politicians serve only as a necessary buffer between the capitalist state—where the real power resides—and the black majority in certain urban and isolated rural jurisdictions. Because black politicians depend so heavily on the decisions of others with real power, they lack the ability to define the political agenda, their horizons are limited, and they have little ability to deliver goods, services, and jobs to their constituents. Thus, according to Marable, there is little reason to expect that African American political incumbents will produce many real improvements for the black community.

Thus, according to those who perceive an American apartheid, racial segregation of African Americans should lead to worse rather than better socioeconomic conditions for that group. Segregation by itself will assure that African Americans are exposed to social and economic conditions far harsher than they would encounter if they were integrated more thoroughly into American society because all-black neighborhoods fall beneath the threshold of stability into disinvestment, abandonment, and commercial decline. Thus the observers who hold this view suggest that high concentrations of African Americans, net of other factors, will compromise African Americans' quality of life.

Given the uncertainty about the outcomes of high concentrations of African American (and, by extension, Latino) neighbors, it is unclear how Empowerment Zone communities will compare with others along several dimensions. Despite a widespread belief that neighborhoods matter in regard to political behavior and other conduct, there is little research demonstrating that neighborhood attributes affect anything other than individual characteristics. Other studies suggest that neighborhoods, in and of themselves, explain little about individuals' political inclinations and actions (e.g., Berry, Portnoy, and Thomson 1991; Guest and Oropesa 1992). Recently, however, social scientists have begun to show that neighborhood characteristics have systematic effects on the behaviors of inner-city residents (e.g., Anderson 1991; Crane 1991a, 1991b) and that neighborhood poverty influences African Americans' public opinions and political participation (e.g., Cohen and Dawson 1993).

In addition to concerns about the racial and socioeconomic composition of neighborhoods, researchers have attempted to assess the impact of neighborhood crime (e.g., Hinz 1994), physical deterioration (Skogan 1990), population density, and the market value of housing stock (King 1975) on various community residents' behaviors, beliefs, and quality of life. Below we use aggregate data from the 1990 U.S. Census and individual survey data from the 1991-1995 Metropolitan Chicago Information Center (MCIC) to present some of the similarities and differences between residents of Empowerment Zone communities and those who live elsewhere in the Chicago area.

Residents of Empowerment Zone Communities and of Others in Chicago

Chicago's Empowerment Zone includes portions of communities on the south and west sides of the city, including Austin, Humboldt Park, East Garfield Park, West Garfield Park, Lower West Lawndale, North Lawndale, South Lawndale, New City, Washington Park, Oakland, Grand Boulevard, Kenwood, and Woodlawn. The Empowerment Zone legislation required that the designated zone have a population of 50,000 to 200,000 residents. The communities in Chicago's Empowerment Zone have a total population of 199,938 persons living in a 14-square-mile area that includes residential neighborhoods, commercial districts, industrial areas, parks, open space, and transportation corridors.

Racially, the Empowerment Zone communities are similar to the Enterprise Communities (ECs) but very different from other Chicago communities (OCCs) and other metro Chicago (OMC) communities. As Figure 3.1 shows, more than seven out of 10 (72%) EZ residents are African American, nearly one out of four (24%) are Hispanic, and fewer than 4% are white. In comparison, six out of 10 (60%) EC residents are African American, 22% are Hispanic, and fewer than one out of six (15%) are white. In other communities in Chicago, fewer than one-fifth of the residents (18%) are African American, 11% are Hispanic, and nearly two-thirds (65%) are white. The racial contrast between residents of the EZ and of the other metro communities is even greater: fewer than one out of 14 (7%) of residents of OMC communities are African American, fewer than 5% are Hispanic, and more than eight out of 10 (84%) are white.

Residents of the EZ also differ economically from others in the metropolitan area. Figure 3.2 shows that almost half (47%) of EZ residents report annual family incomes of less than $20,000; the mean family income for residents in the zone is less than $24,000. About three out of 10 (29%) residents of the EC report family incomes of less than $20,000, and their average family income is just over $25,000. By contrast, other Chicago residents have mean family incomes of more than $40,000; fewer than one-fifth (18%) have family incomes below $20,000. Those outside the city have average family incomes of more than $53,000; fewer than one out of 10 (9%) report family incomes below $20,000.

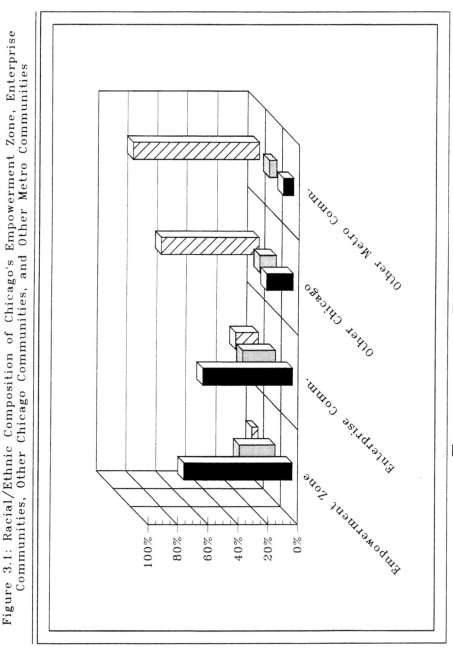

Figure 3.1: Racial/Ethnic Composition of Chicago's Empowerment Zone, Enterprise Communities, Other Chicago Communities, and Other Metro Communities

■ African American □ Latino ⊠ White

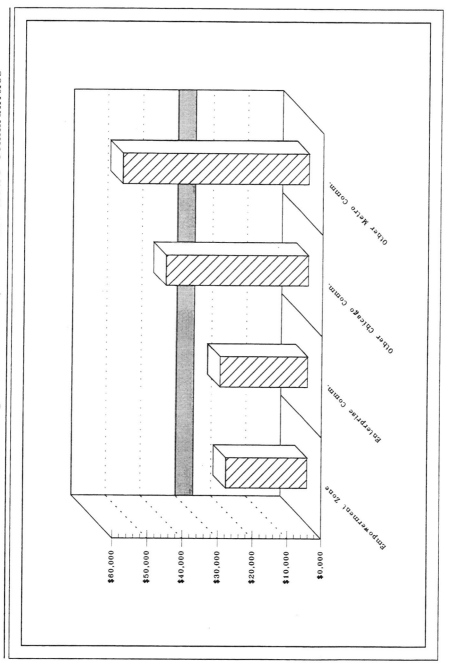

Figure 3.2: Mean Family Incomes in Chicago's Empowerment Zone, Enterprise Communities, Other Chicago Communities, and Other Metro Communities

Figure 3.3 shows other selected characteristics of EZ, EC, OCC, and OMC communities. For each area, the chart shows the percentage of community residents who are high school graduates, the percentage who receive welfare, the percentage unemployed, the percentage with professional or managerial employment, and the percentage who are homeowners. Generally this chart shows that EZ communities are more similar to Enterprise Communities than to other Chicago communities and to other communities outside the city.

Figure 3.3 shows that only half of the residents of Chicago's Empowerment Zone have completed high school (or more), a lower proportion than in all other parts of the metropolitan area: 61% of the residents of the Enterprise Communities, more than 70% of other Chicago residents, and more than 85% of those outside the city have completed at least high school.

This figure also suggests that one-third of residents in the Empowerment Zone receive Aid to Families with Dependent Children, as opposed to 17% of residents of the Enterprise Communities, fewer than 7% of those from other Chicago communities, and 2% of those from areas outside Chicago. About one out of eight (12.3%) residents of the Empowerment Zone are unemployed, in contrast to 8.5% of the residents of Enterprise Communities, 5.6% of other Chicago residents, and 2.4% of non-Chicago residents.

Figure 3.3 also presents the percentage of professional and managerial workers who live in each of the areas. Fewer than one out of five (18.6%) Empowerment Zone residents are professional or managerial workers, as opposed to 22% of the residents of the Enterprise Communities, 34% of other Chicago residents, and 36% of those living outside Chicago.

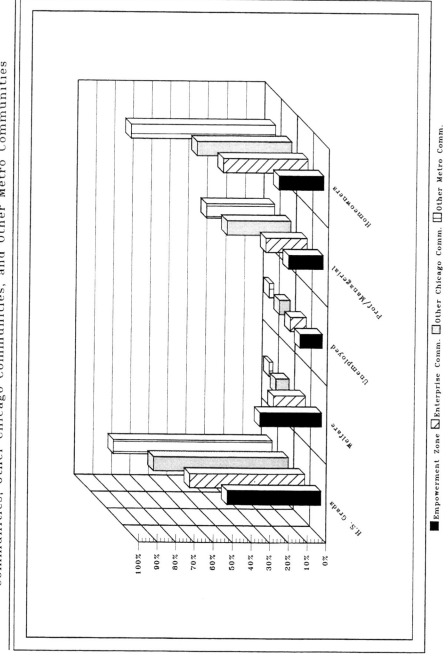

Figure 3.3: Selected Characteristics of Chicago's Empowerment Zone, Enterprise Communities, Other Chicago Communities, and Other Metro Communities

Home ownership in the Empowerment Zone is substantially lower than in other areas: Fewer than one-fourth (24%) of EZ residents own their home, in contrast to 45% of EC residents, 50% of other Chicago residents, and 77% of those living outside Chicago.

Do residents of Empowerment Zones differ socially from others? Several indicators could be used to answer this question. We use criteria such as going to local festivals, visiting museums, attending sporting events, going to plays, concerts, or the theater, and visiting locations such as zoos, aquariums, and amusement parks. Figure 3.4 presents the percentage of residents of the various areas who go to local festivals. Slightly larger proportions of EZ residents than of EC residents report attending such festivals, but smaller proportions of EZ residents attend than do residents of other Chicago-area communities. This figure also shows that a smaller proportion of EZ residents than of others have visited museums, and smaller proportions of EZ and EC residents than of others have witnessed professional sporting events.

Figure 3.5 displays the percentages of residents of the various areas who have gone to plays, zoos, aquariums, or amusement parks. With the exception of visiting amusement parks, EZ residents are less likely than others to have reported such experiences. These lower levels of participation are not due to a lack of free time: Residents of EZs are more likely than others to say that they have more free time these days.

Figure 3.4: Percentage of Chicago's Empowerment Zone, Enterprise Communities, Other Chicago Communities, and Other Metro Communities Who Have Visited Various Locations

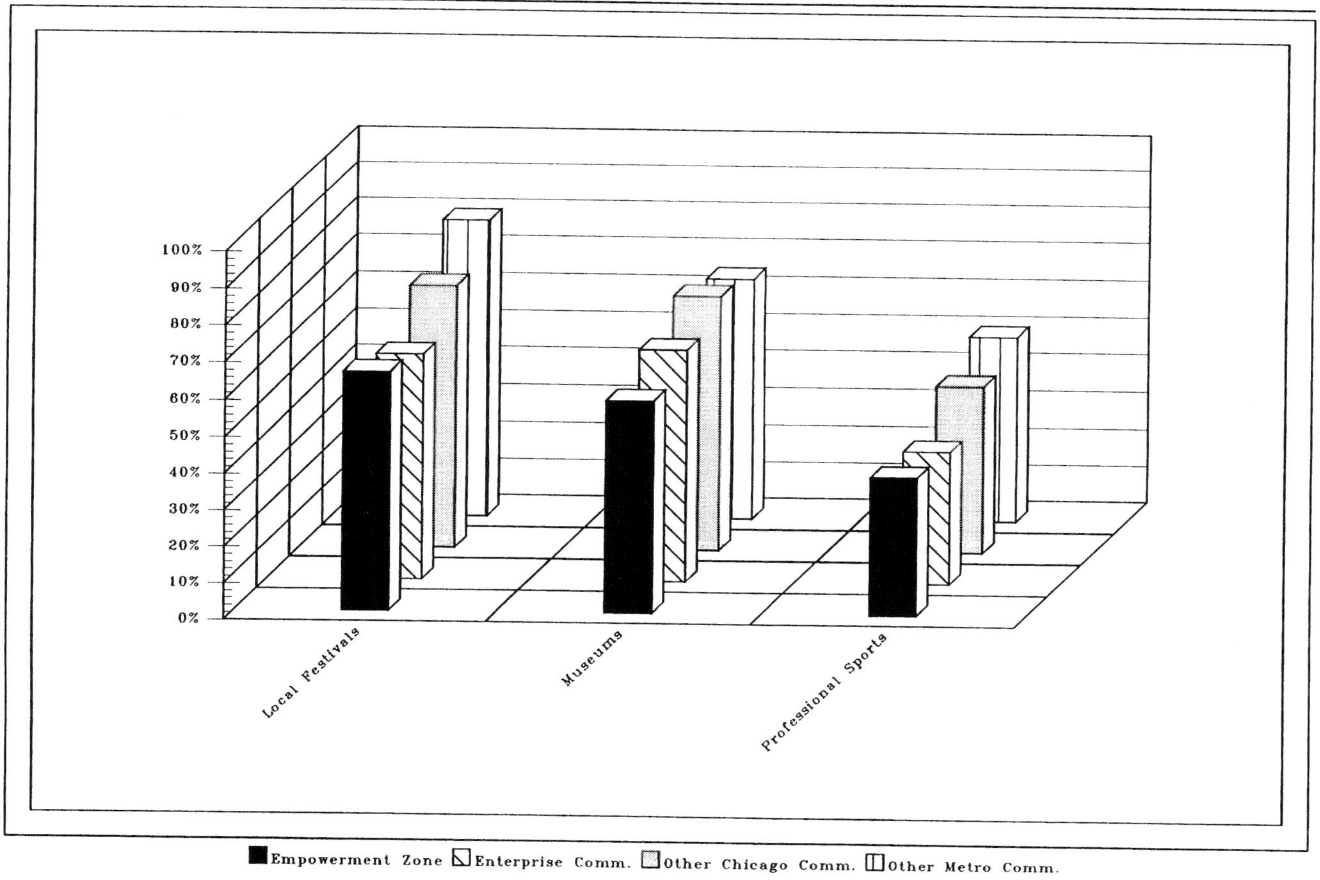

Figure 3.5: Percentage of Chicago's Empowerment Zone, Enterprise Communities, Other Chicago Communities, and Other Metro Communities Who Have Visited Various Locations

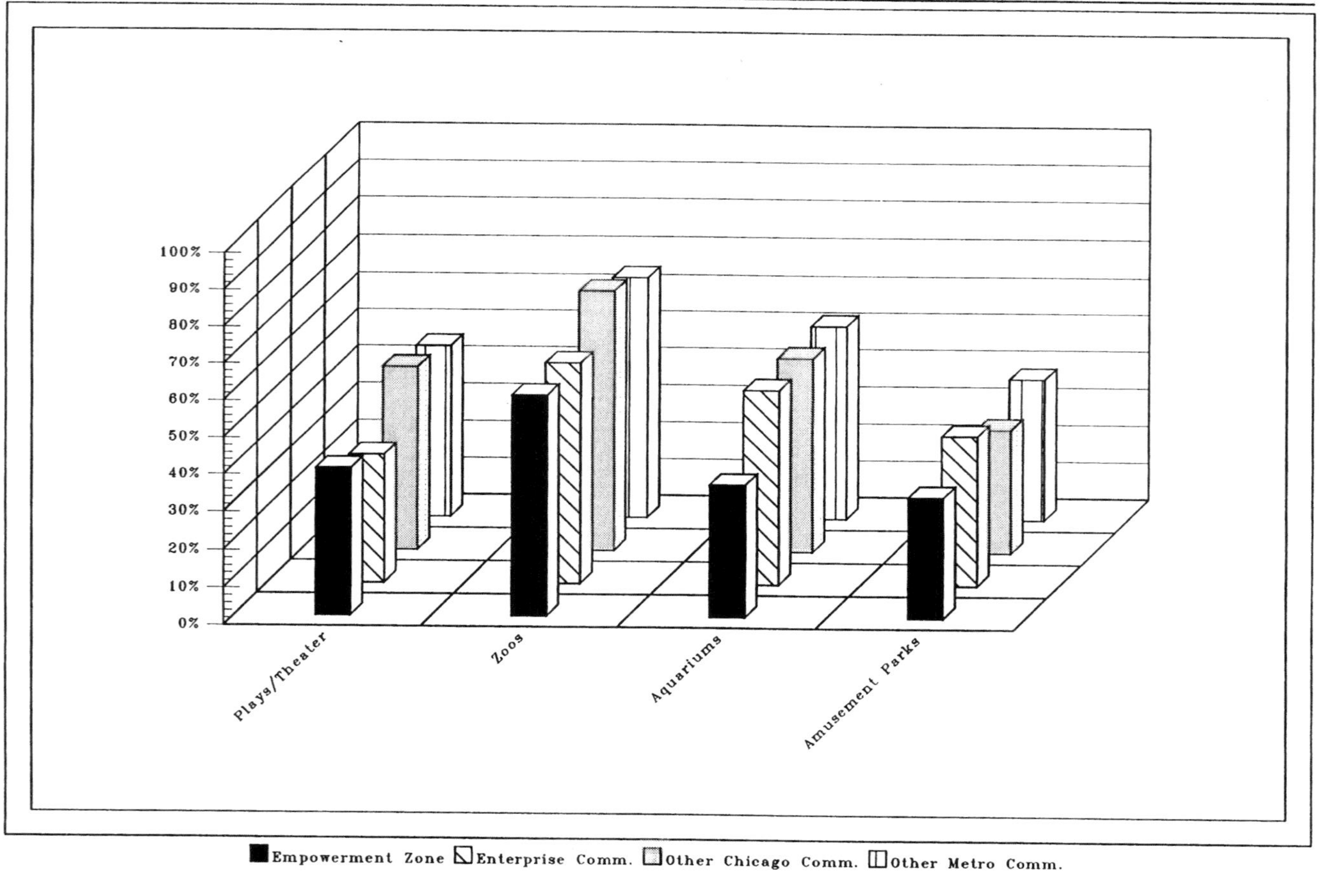

Generally these results suggest that Empowerment Zone residents are less socially engaged than other people in the Chicago area. On most activities, they are even less fully engaged than residents of Enterprise Communities. There is reason to believe that these depressed levels of social participation reflect the economic difference between EZ residents and others in the metropolitan area.

Are residents of Empowerment Zones able to overcome their economic circumstances and become as involved in political participation as others in the metropolitan area? Political participation can be defined as any action or gesture that seeks to influence, support, or undermine the activities of those who make decisions about matters of distribution. Such involvement is not one-dimensional; there are several styles or modes of political participation or involvement. Moreover, as Milbrath (1981) points out, people might engage in countless specific political behaviors. Some people might join extremist social movements; others might write letters to their congress members, read literature printed by alternative political parties, withhold their votes, campaign more fervently for those they believe will better serve their political interests, or drop out of political activities altogether.

According to Milbrath, communicators are likely to engage in the following activities: staying informed about politics, sending messages of support to political leaders when they are doing well, sending protest messages to political leaders when they are doing badly, engaging in political discussions, informing others in their communities about politics, making their views known to public officials, writing letters to the editors of newspapers, or participating in other activities that require interchange between the individual and other members of his or her community.

Community activists are identified as people with high degrees of involvement in public matters and societal issues. These actors form groups to deal with social problems, work with existing groups to confront such problems, contact public officials about issues that go beyond strictly personal or familial concerns, are active in organizations concerned with public issues, and engage in undertakings that would improve the conditions of their community or social group. These activists differ from party and campaign workers in the sense that their activities are not exclusively or even primarily aimed at the formal, electoral political process. Community activists are far less concerned with party and campaign politics than are party activists. One can distinguish among community activists by asking what kinds of actions they participate in and how frequently they participate.

Figure 3.6 indicates the extent and type of involvement in various kinds of political participation among residents of Chicago's Empowerment Zone and residents of other areas. This figure shows that EZ residents are as likely as others in the Chicago metropolitan area (if not slightly more so) to report that they are registered to vote. More than eight out of 10 (81%) EZ residents report that they are currently registered, in comparison with 83% of EC residents, 79% of other Chicago residents, and 80% of non-Chicago residents.

Similarly, EZ residents are more likely than others to report that they are affiliated with a political party. As Figure 3.7 shows, 68% of EZ residents report a party affiliation, as compared with 67% of EC residents, 60% of other Chicago residents, and 55% of non-Chicago residents.

Figure 3.6: Percentage of Residents in Chicago's Empowerment Zone, Enterprise Communities, Other Chicago Communities, and Other Metro Communities Who Are Registered to Vote

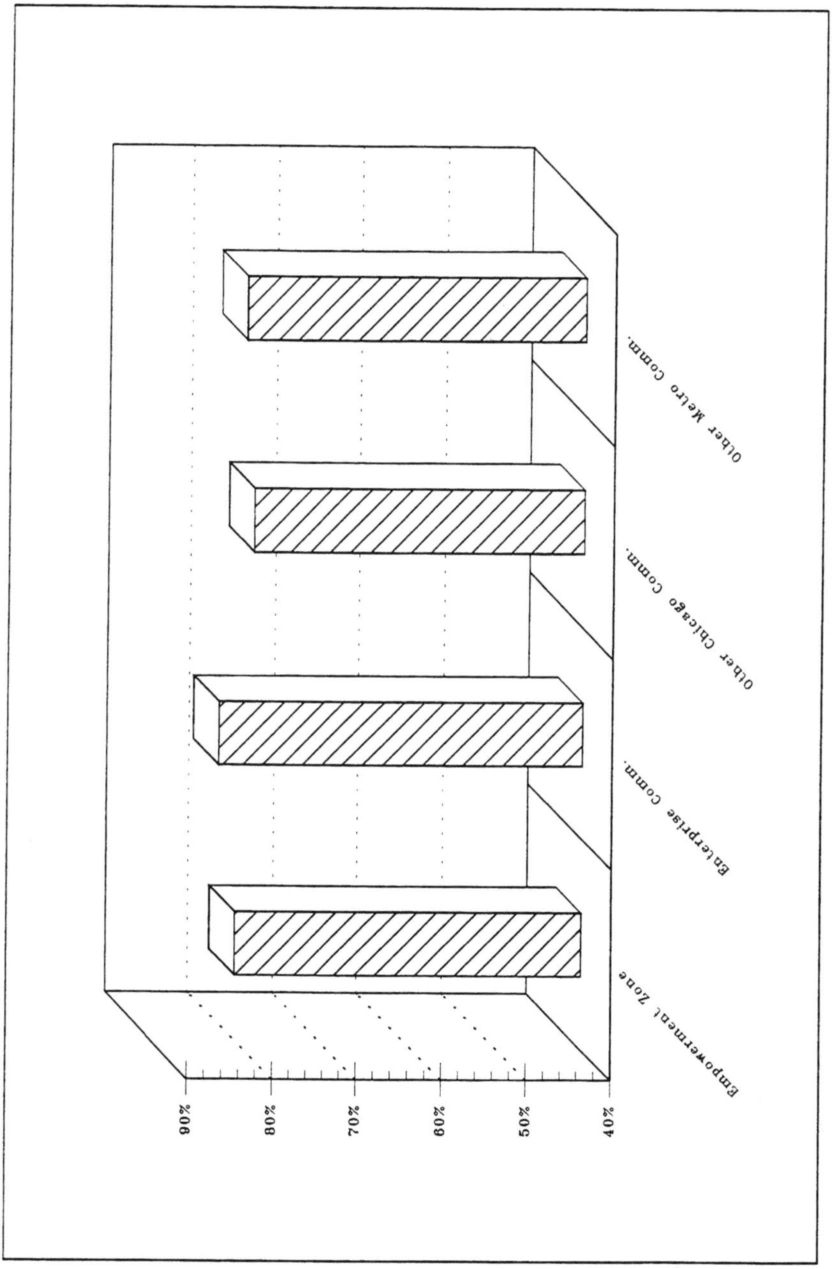

Figure 3.7: Percentage of Residents in Chicago's Empowerment Zone, Enterprise Communities, Other Chicago Communities, and Other Metro Communities With a Party Affiliation

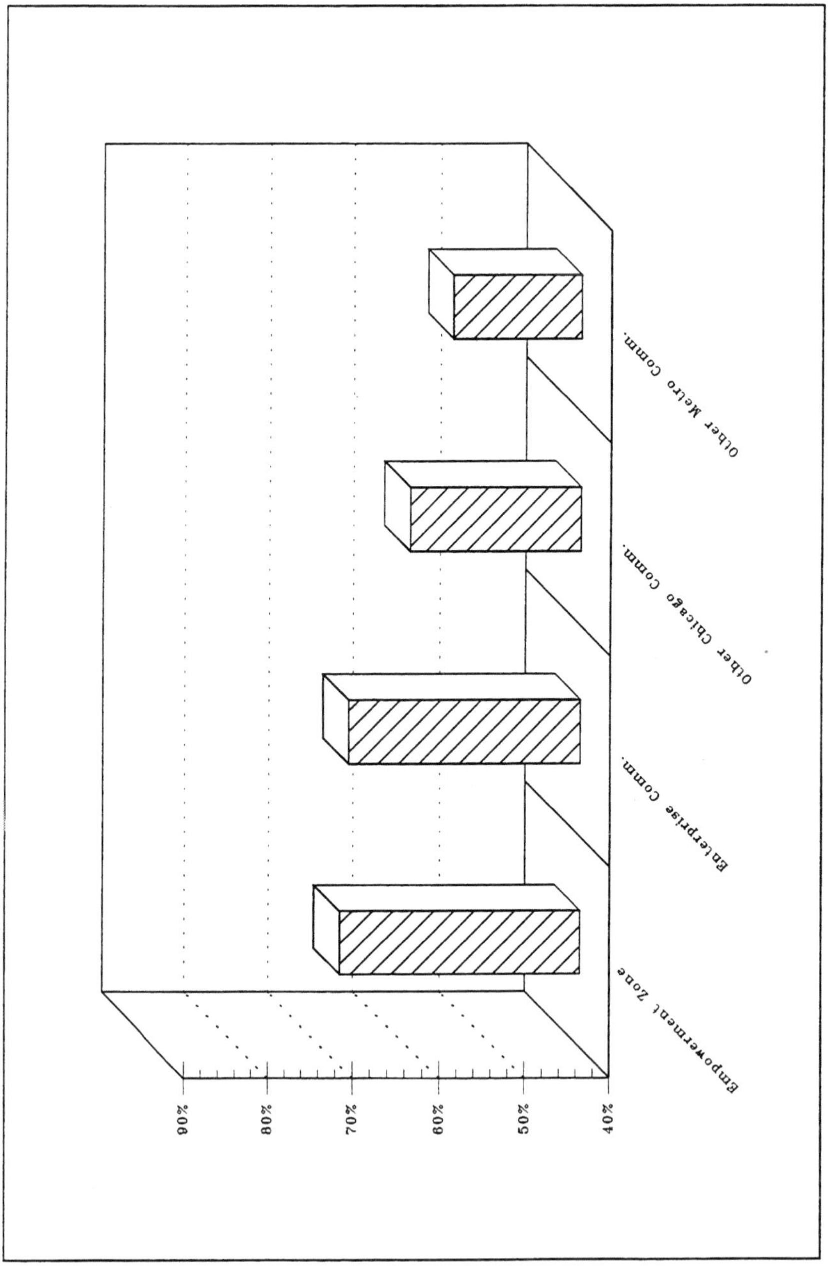

Figure 3.8 also shows that EZ and EC residents are more likely than others to report contacting public officials about neighborhood problems. Fewer than 10% of non-Chicago residents report that they have contacted public officials; 19% of EZ and EC residents have done so. This is true even though EZ (3%) and EC (2%) residents are no more likely than other Chicago residents (2%) and other metro residents (5%) to report bad government services in their neighborhoods.

In keeping with the idea that Empowerment Zone residents have elevated levels of political participation, they are more likely than all but the EC residents to belong to neighborhood associations and community organizations. Figure 3.9 shows that 18% of EZ residents and 22% of EC residents belong to such associations, as compared with 13% of other Chicago residents and 12% of non-Chicago residents.

These results tend to suggest that Empowerment Zone residents are more politically active than all others except EC residents, despite the lower economic status of these communities and the lower levels of social engagement among the residents.

Despite higher levels of political participation, however, some critics (as mentioned previously) suggest that that inner cities represent concentrations of poverty and social problems, not of power. It is possible,

Figure 3.8: Percentage of Residents in Chicago's Empowerment Zone, Enterprise Communities, Other Chicago Communities, and Other Metro Communities Who Have Contacted Public Officials

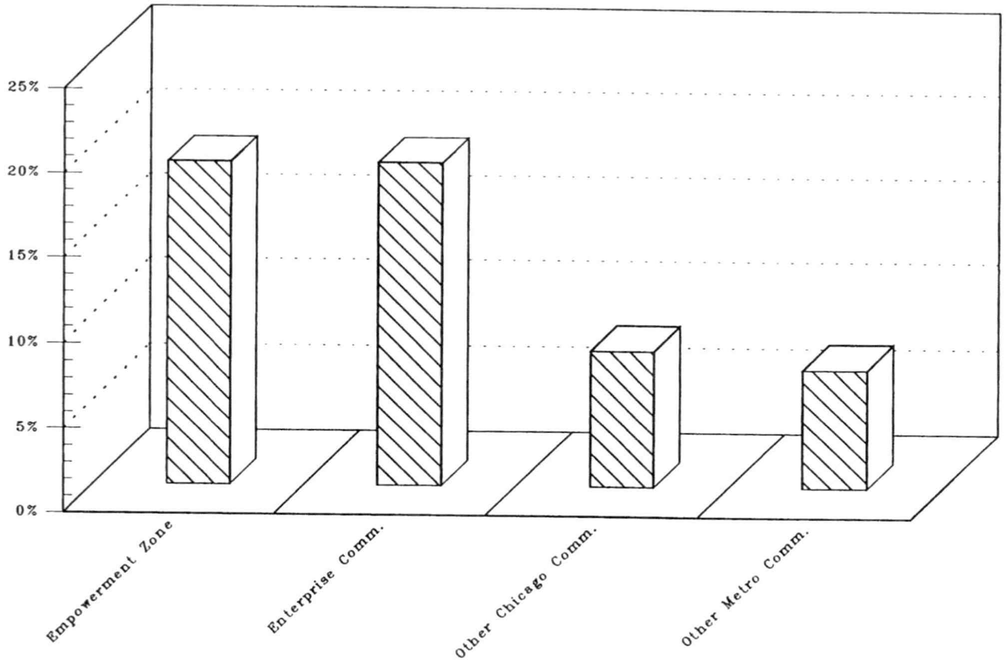

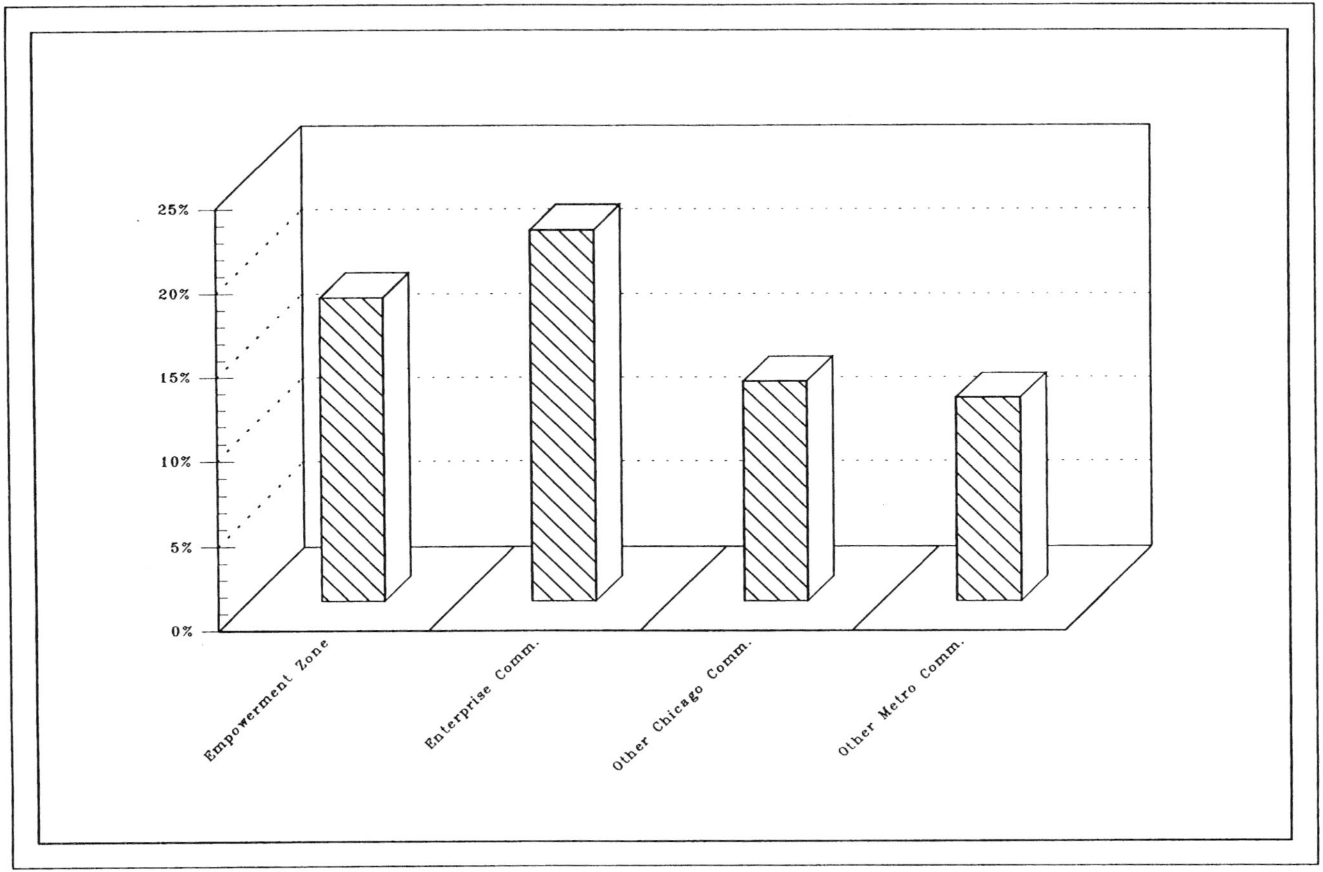

Figure 3.9: Percentage of Residents in Chicago's Empowerment Zone, Enterprise Communities, Other Chicago Communities, and Other Metro Communities Who Belong to Neighborhood Organizations

that segregated neighborhoods concentrate self-destructive behaviors in ways that are likely to offset any empowering effects.

Figures 3.10 and 3.11 present information about the perceptions of social problems held by people who live in the various areas. Figure 3.10 shows that EZ residents are far more likely than all others to report that there is "a lot" of crime in their neighborhoods: 42% of EZ residents hold this perception, in contrast to 26% of EC residents, 17% of other Chicago residents, and 4% of other metro area residents. More than one-fourth (26%) of EZ residents say that their neighborhoods have high crime rates and are unsafe; fewer than one out of 13 (7%) of those living outside Chicago report such concerns. Similarly, one-fourth (25%) of EZ residents report dissatisfaction with gang activity in their neighborhoods, in contrast to one out of 20 (5%) of those living outside Chicago.

According to Figure 3.11, nearly four out of 10 (39%) of EZ residents report that their neighborhoods have become worse places to live over the past five years, as opposed to 13% of those living outside Chicago. Similarly, more than half (56%) of EZ residents report vacant buildings in their neighborhoods; fewer than 4% of those living outside Chicago report such vacancies.

The evidence in these figures suggests that Empowerment Zones in fact contain concentrations of social problems and disinvestment. These areas have higher perceived rates of crime, greater dissatisfaction with gang activities, more widespread perceptions of worsening neighborhood conditions, and greater numbers of abandoned buildings.

not new...

92

Figure 3.10: Perceptions of Neighborhood Security Among Residents of Chicago's Empowerment Zone, Enterprise Communities, Other Chicago Communities, and Other Metro Communities

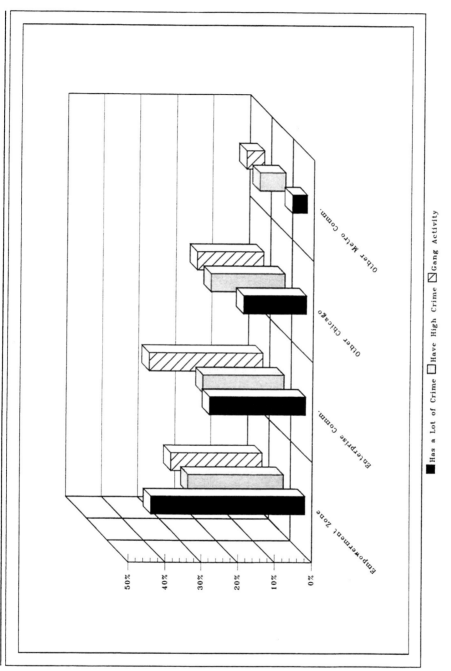

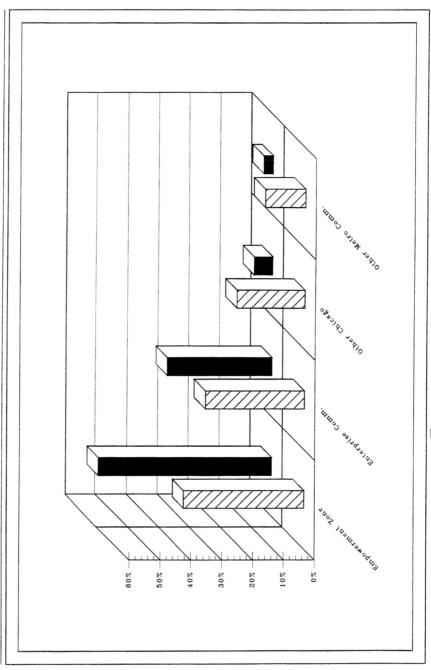

Figure 3.11: Perceptions of Neighborhood Conditions Among Residents of Chicago's Empowerment Zone, Enterprise Communities, Other Chicago Communities, and Other Metro Communities

In sum, it appears that Chicago's Empowerment Zone is consistent with the expectations of the Empowerment Zone legislation: It is composed of neighborhoods that are economically depressed but politically engaged. The residents, however, are less engaged socially than others in the Chicago area. Residents of Empowerment Zones are also more likely than others to regard their communities as permeated with social problems such as high crime, gangs, and disinvestment.

and the point is?

Summary and Conclusions

We began this chapter with the observation that the national Empowerment Zone legislation calls for some seemingly opposing conditions: high levels of poverty and high rates of political activism in communities with high levels of social problems. These apparently contradictory expectations are based on the premise that in healthy communities, residents themselves must identify and address problems, share information, and work toward their common goals. Thus, grassroots activism and the potential for mobilization are necessary ingredients for any "empowerment"-based strategies to combat poverty and social problems.

These policies are also based on the fact that a "one size fits all" orientation cannot work in such a wide variety of communities. Because the challenges facing urban America are varied and complex, no single policy can resolve all the issues. In all cases, however, urban policies must seek to build bridges from distressed communities to economic opportunity.

Chicago's Empowerment Zone communities differ socially, politically, and economically from other communities in the Chicago metropolitan area. EZ communities are typically more economically distressed than others, and the residents generally are less socially engaged than residents of other areas; yet, they are also more politically involved. Because of this combination of traits, an infusion of resources into Chicago's Empowerment Zone communities might lead to local initiatives to combat violent crime, joblessness, abandoned buildings, drug abuse and dealing, and other social ills that currently undermine the economic vitality of these communities.

In addition, political empowerment among African Americans has been correlated with outcomes such as improvements in health, reductions in political alienation, and greater access to jobs in the government sector. Yet, high concentrations of African Americans (which often make political empowerment possible) also have corresponded to high concentrations of poverty rather than power. These concentrations of poverty are accompanied by the loss of civic and commercial services to the segregated neighborhood in the form of declining retail demand, increasing residential abandonment, business disinvestment, deindustrialization, and massive job loss. Therefore, one of the challenges is to find empowerment solutions that do not rely on racial segregation as a means of creating empowerment.

Similarly, urban policies geared toward economic development must reject the false choice between empowering poor people and revitalizing distressed communities. Both kinds of assistance will be needed to assist the residents in their bottom-up efforts to rebuild their neighborhoods. Community residents and others must invest in the physical revitalization of troubled areas; reconstruction efforts will not be truly successful unless the people they seek to serve are fully engaged in the design and execution of redevelopment plans. Empowerment Zones in Chicago appear to provide the potential for such circumstances.

Chapter 4

A Chronology of Chicago's Empowerment Zone Process

Noah Temaner Jenkins and Kathy Feingold

I t is always dangerous to rush to judgment about recent events. As Gittell and colleagues (1996:40) point out, "[T]oo often we judge program efforts to create social change so early that we preclude the possibility of finding outcomes. Failing to find results after one, two or three years, we declare the program a failure and abandon it or disparage it so severely that it is strangled by lack of support." A far greater risk, however, is waiting until events have unfolded completely and then providing irrelevant analysis after the fact. Analysis of the Empowerment Zone effort may well suffer from irrelevance if it is not conducted in a timely fashion so that it can be used to redirect aspects that are going astray.

We believe it is important to understand the role of events in the course of the Empowerment Zone process. Below we outline some of the critical events of the early phase of the Empowerment Zone process in Chicago. "Critical events" are consequential turning points or discrete developments in a process that predispose subsequent actions to follow identifiable lines. Critical events provide some qualitative change at a specific point in time and limit the options for the outcomes. In studying political outcomes, one must understand the role of such events in determining the actors' possible range of choices.

While others may suggest other events that have been important to the Empowerment Zone process, we offer this list to those who wish to understand how political circumstances and institutions have helped shape the implementation of the Empowerment Zone legislation in Chicago.

Chronology of Events

August 10, 1993	Omnibus Budget Reconciliation Act of 1993 designates the creation of 6 urban Empowerment Zones, 3 rural Empowerment Zones, and 65 Enterprise Communities.
September 9, 1993	The President creates the Community Empowerment Board (CEB), to coordinate interdepartmental activity among federal agencies.
Summer 1993 - **January 1994**	The City of Chicago Departments of Planning and Development, Health and Aging, Environment, Housing, the Mayor's Office for People with Disabilities and others begin to meet to discuss the Empowerment Zone concept and organize to participate in the Federal competition.
	Chicago community activists and development coalitions become involved in designing the Empowerment Zone initiative by combining the Enterprise Zone approach with a community empowerment dimension.

December 1993 -
January 1994   A task force of community and human development practitioners and
                            CDC executives is convened by the University of Illinois at
                            Chicago's Center for Urban Economic Development (UICUED) and
                            the Community Workshop on Economic Development (CWED),
                            with the assistance of the Women's Self-Employment Project
                            (WSEP) to prepare a briefing paper to the Clinton Transition Team
                            and Secretary-elect of HUD, Henry Cisneros. This paper addresses
                            what could be done in central cities to make current programs under
                            existing Congressional authorizations more effective, responsive,
                            and promote community development goals. The briefing paper
                            recommends administrative exemptions, regulatory waivers, and
                            other modifications to address welfare to work reforms, the Job
                            Training Partnership Act (JTPA)/employment development and the
                            extension of the Enterprise Zone concept to the inner city.

January 18, 1994   The Community Workshop on Economic Development (CWED)
                            holds a legislative briefing for elected officials in Washington, D.C.
                            on the provisions of the EZ regulations.

January 18, 1994   Federal Register details the rules and regulations of applying for an
                            Empowerment Zone or Enterprise Community.

January - April 1994   Local communities are mobilized to apply for inclusion in the
                            Empowerment Zone application. Each community that wants to be
                            part of the EZ has to prepare a strategic plan. The City declares its
                            intention to submit at least one Empowerment Zone application. The
                            City Department of Planning and Development begins to serve as the
                            lead city agency.

February 3, 1994   Vice President Al Gore presents Empowerment Zone concept at the
                            Westin Hotel in Chicago and at Lucy Flower High School on the
                            Westside. Flower High's Youth Enterprise Network had been cited
                            as a model approach to urban revitalization through comprehensive
                            development planning and community involvement with government
                            and the private sector.

February 9, 1994 An information session is held to provide an opportunity for city-wide organizations to discuss possible roles and involvement for community organizations and government entities in EZ/EC activities and also to review program regulations. The session draws over 400 participants.

February 16, 1994 The City of Chicago's first official informational session is held at Harold Washington Library and sponsored by Mayor Daley to introduce EZ program to the city, identify benefits to community, set forth eligibility requirements to participation, and begin a dialogue between the city and public. Called the "Community Kick-Off."

February 1994 The Mayor appoints a 30 member board, consisting of government, private industry, and city-wide community development professionals, to develop a process to select the geographic boundaries for the EZ/EC applications and coordinate the development of the strategic plan.

February 18, 1994 An EZ Task Force planning session held at University of Illinois at Chicago, sponsored by the Great Cities Initiative.

February 22, 1994 City-wide EZ/EC informational and planning meeting at the Community Workshop on Economic Development (CWED).

February 26, 1994 CWED and UIC Great Cities, with the support of the City of Chicago Department of Planning and Development, co-host a meeting of over 100 representatives of community-based organizations culminating a series of informational and planning meetings. Selection criteria and processes are determined for nominating EZ and EC community entities.

March 1, 1994 The Urban Land Institute holds a meeting to develop strategies for involving the business community.

March 9-22, 1994	City of Chicago sponsors a series of community meetings, two each on the west, south, and far south sides of the city.
March 22, 1994	EZ Request for Statement of Interest and Qualifications forms are available. Communities interested in being a part of Chicago's applicant EZ must submit a proposal including their own strategic plans.
April 7, 1994	Community proposals due to DPD. Thirty-three proposals are submitted, and applicants are scheduled to orally present their proposals to the Coordinating Council and the public.
April 13, 1994	Chicago Empowerment Zone Ordinances are passed by City Council authorizing application for designation of Empowerment Zone and Enterprise Communities.
April 15 & 16, 1994	Public presentations of proposals.
May 2, 1994	Boundary selection announced. Eleven applications are selected, determining most of the boundaries and providing the basis for the Empowerment Zone strategic plan.
May 6, 1994	City sponsored city-wide meeting.
May 7, 1994	City sponsored city-wide meeting at Malcolm X College where community organizers asked city representatives to leave the room so they could discuss their involvement in the zone. In a 45 minute session, the 200 people present agreed to work together to make sure the residents are able to contribute substantially to the EZ application.
May 18, 1994	The map of the EZ boundaries ratified by the Chicago City Council. The area selected is a non-contiguous zone with 199,938 people and 14.3 square miles. This includes parts of the west side, near west, and the mid-south side. Also included are three areas applying for Enterprise Community status, one west, south and far south.

Spring 1994   The proposed EZ and EC areas, called clusters, elect a Joint Empowerment Zone/Enterprising Communities Governance Council that has ten members from each of the three clusters and two members from each of the Enterprise Communities. This is to promote cooperation and communication among the Chicago EZ and EC clusters.

May 1994   New Coordinating Council established by the Mayor. Fifteen initial members step down to be replaced by 15 community participants who worked on the community proposals.

May-June 1994   Coordinating Council members, and city staff and their hired writing consultants write the strategic plan based on the community proposals and ideas discussed at public meetings.

June 4, 1994   Public presentation of strategic plan prepared by DPD staff.

June 10, 1994   Community representatives and city officials meet at CWED to discuss the draft. Community representatives feel it does not represent their views and want certain concepts explicitly detailed. The draft was edited to reflect these wishes.

June 28, 1994   Mayor, Governor and Community sign the four-volume Empowerment Zone application which includes the strategic plan and the Enterprise Community applications from the City of Chicago.

June 30, 1994   Federal due date for all Empowerment Zone applications.

July - November 1994   The (interim) EZ/EC Coordinating Council creates five standing committees: 1) the Committee on Plan Development to oversee the refinement of the strategic plan, 2) the Committee on Marketing and Outreach to develop a program for increasing public and private participation and resources in the zone, 3) the Committee on Reinventing Government to develop a governance structure that responds to community recommendations, identify mechanisms for

distribution of funds in conjunction with the Resources Development Committee, create a mechanism for identifying new areas for waiver requests and program changes, and evaluate the effectiveness of local government and the cluster groups in responding to the community's needs; 4) the Committee on Resource Development to attract additional funding sources in cooperation with the reinventing government committee; and 5) the Committee on Operations to identify and implement logistical requirements for highly visible projects and create opportunities for workshops for
community participants and city staff, create an EZ/EC evaluation system for ongoing program evaluation, and work with technical advisors identified by the Resource Development Committee.

Cluster activity centers on developing a governance process and initiating implementation plans, including establishing Initiative Task Forces to refine the community proposals and reconcile them with the EZ strategic plan. Clusters meet with DPD staff to refine "fast track" projects that could be implemented within the first 100 days.

During this time EZ Clusters hold local community conventions, assemblies, forums and informational sessions focusing on the content of the strategic plan and Cluster priorities.

July 12, 1994

The City and the EZ/EC CC send a delegation to Washington, D.C. to meet with the Illinois Congressional Delegation and key HUD officials.

December 12, 1994

The Commissioner of Planning and Development for the City of Chicago submits, at the request of HUD, supplemental information to the Empowerment Zone proposal.

December 21, 1994

Chicago is designated as a federal urban Empowerment Zone along with Atlanta, Baltimore, Detroit, New York, and the bi-state partnership of Philadelphia and Camden. None of Chicago's EC applicants are designated.

January 12, 1995   Final Rules and Regulations on Designation of Empowerment Zones and Enterprise Communities published in the Federal Register.

January 13, 1995   The community Joint Governance Council sends a letter to Mayor Richard M. Daley responding to the supplemental information for the Chicago Empowerment Zone application that the Commissioner of Planning and Development submitted to HUD on December 12, 1994 without the review of the EZ/EC Joint Governance Council. The JGC letter requests that "...no official actions by the City of Chicago be undertaken... [without] full participation, collaboration, review and approval [of the Joint Governance Council and the Coordinating Council] of all decisions affecting EZ designation."

April 13, 1995   The City Department of Planning and Development puts forth an ordinance stating the membership, powers and duties, and nomination procedures for the permanent EZ/EC Coordinating Council. According to this, the composition of the Council is to be twelve community representatives, including three from each EZ Cluster and one from each EC Cluster; ten representatives of business located either inside or outside the zone; ten government, including one state and one county appointee, one representative of Chicago's Department of Planning and Development, and seven other local government agency representatives; and seven at-large members. All CC members will be Mayoral appointments, except the county and state representatives.

April-June 1995   Some community representatives resist this ordinance because it deviates from the structure proposed in the strategic plan, and drastically reduces the level of community participation on the EZ/EC CC. An alternate ordinance, also known as the "People's Ordinance," that more closely represents the structure described in the strategic plan is prepared by South Cluster community participants, but never accepted as the governing structure. The governance structure presented in the strategic plan was identified in the document as "a starting point," which never developed further.

May 10-12, 1995	Strategic Implementation Workshop in Washington, D.C. Detroit, Chicago, Atlanta and Cleveland participate.
June 14, 1995	As a result of pressure from community advocates, the DPD draft ordinance is revised to include three more community representatives, with two fewer at-large and one less business representative. It also requires that six of the business representatives be from businesses in the zone. It does, however, reserve appointments for the Mayor. This is approved by the Mayor and the City Council. Composition will be 15 community representatives, including four from each EZ Cluster and one from each EC Cluster; six zone business representatives; ten government representatives, including one state and one county appointee, one representative of Chicago's Department of Planning and Development, and seven other local government agency representatives; three at-large business representatives; and five at-large representatives.
June 28, 1995	Request for nominations for the permanent EZ/EC Coordinating Council members released.
July-August 1995	The EZ/EC CC focuses on developing a request for proposals (RFP) to allocate the HHS grant money. The Plan Development subcommittee has a series of meetings with Chicago DPD to frame the process and reach consensus on content of the RFP. They agree that city staff will provide technical reviews of proposals and the EZ/EC CC will assess the policy merits of proposals. Overall, the review process should ensure each proposal is consistent with the strategic plan and individual Cluster plans.
July 31, 1995	Nominations for the permanent EZ/EC Coordinating Council due.
August 30, 1995	HUD sponsors a Washington, D.C. conference, "Strategies for Success."

Community activists from urban EZs and Enhanced Enterprise Communities (EECs) gather in Lisle, Illinois and agree to establish a national consortium of EZs and EECs as a first step in developing a national organization of all designees, and possibly all EZ/EC applicants. The Consortium will share information, provide mutual assistance, pursue funding to support resident participation and influence national urban policy.

September 29, 1995   Memorandum of Agreement (MOA) is signed by the Federal Department of Housing and Urban Development, the State of Illinois, and the City of Chicago at a public meeting with about 50 people attending.

October 19, 1995   Request for Proposals (RFP), developed by the Plan Development Committee of the EZ/EC CC, is approved by the full EZ/EC CC and officially released. Pre-application conference is held at Dunbar Vocational School to provide information about the RFP. Meeting attended by city department heads to provide guidance in preparing proposals.

October 25-
November 7, 1995   Community meetings held in the clusters to prepare those interested in submitting proposals.

November 8, 1995   Permanent EZ/EC Coordinating Council is appointed, with members to serve for two years.

December 15, 1995   Permanent EZ/EC CC meets for orientation. Member handbook is distributed.

December 18, 1995   Proposals due, and 242 are submitted.

December 20 & 27, 1995   Ad Hoc Group on Ethics and Organization of the EZ/EC CC meet to develop specific recommendations for the Coordinating Council to consider at its first meeting.

January 5, 1996	First EZ/EC CC meeting. Members nominate themselves for committees.
January 12, 1996	Second EZ/EC meeting. Members are elected to four standing committees: 1) Executive Committee; 2) Committee on Community and Business Outreach; 3) Committee on Policy and Planning; and 4) Committee on Finance.
February 21-23, 1996	HUD sponsors "Partnerships in Action" conference in Washington, D.C. for EZ and EC participants.
March 6, 1996	First group of 16 proposals, already approved by the Coordinating Council, introduced to City Council for about $8.1 million in Empowerment Zone funding.
March 19, 1996	President Clinton proposes a second round of Empowerment Zone and Enterprise Community designations.
June 1996	Senators Carol Moseley-Braun (D-IL) and Charles Rangel (D-NY) introduce to Congress the Community Empowerment Act. This would allow for the designation of 20 more Empowerment Zones and 80 more Enterprise Communities, along with a new set of tax incentives.
July 31, 1996	Second group of 58 approved proposals introduced to City Council for about $29 million more in Empowerment Zone funds.
December 1996	First contracts with grantees are signed.
January 14, 1997	Eleven more approved projects introduced to City Council. These are the last of the proposals. At this point, all proposals have either been approved or rejected by the Coordinating Council, and they begin discussions on the next round of grants.

Chapter 5

Citizen Participation in Chicago's Empowerment Process

The Application for Empowerment Zone and Enterprise Community Status

Michelle L. Story-Stewart, Mark Sendzik, and Anna Marie Schuh

The Empowerment Zone/Enterprise Community legislation evolved from a combination of the Republican Enterprise Zone concept of the 1980s and the Model Cities program of the 1960s. The former offers businesses tax incentives to locate in economically depressed areas, in the belief that the benefits will trickle down to residents. The latter was a Democratic initiative that required citizen participation in creating redevelopment strategies for poor urban areas.

The 1993 legislation provided for nine Empowerment Zones and ninety-five Enterprise Communities. It limited the population in each Empowerment Zone to the lesser of ten percent of the city population or 200,000 people and the land area to 20 square miles. These limitations were significant for Chicago, which covers more than 70 square miles and where more than 1 million residents were estimated to be eligible under the poverty criteria.

The Empowerment Zone (EZ) legislation is unique in that it targets poor neighborhoods with tax breaks and increased social program spending, but also requires comprehensive community planning, significant participation by citizens, and partnerships among community, government, and the private sector.

The legislation highlighted the concept of citizen participation, and President Clinton stressed that not a single dollar would be spent without a coordinated strategy developed at the grassroots level. Because the Clinton administration attempted to solicit input from community-based organizations (CBOs) before proposing regulations, this grassroots effort started in Chicago before the application process officially began. Many Chicago communities became aware of the Empowerment Zone opportunity in October 1993 through informational mailings from the Community Workshop on Economic Development (CWED) or a discussion about the effort at CWED's annual membership meeting. In January 1994, CWED initiated informational community meetings, and at that point many communities began to explore potential Empowerment Zone activities. This was the beginning of a strong bottom-up movement pursued on a track parallel with the city's efforts.

Because so many areas of Chicago were eligible on the basis of need guidelines and were already developing community plans, it was important to open up to the communities the process of determining the geographic boundaries of the proposed zone. Eventually, the mayor appointed an interim Empowerment Zone/Enterprise Community Coordinating Council (EZ/EC CC) to conduct the application process, with significant community participation.

The EZ/EC CC notified communities about the opportunity to nominate sites for inclusion in the Chicago application. Interested communities submitted statements of interest to the EZ/EC CC for approval. These statements, or feeder applications, were used to allow the respective communities to participate in assessing the needs and assets of their areas. Information from these documents would be used later in the Chicago application to the federal government.

Finally, the EZ/EC CC evaluated the 33 submissions in light of the HUD requirements to narrow the list of Chicago application areas. Then a writing committee composed of city officials, consultants hired by the city, and a substantial number of community members wrote the application.

The committee decided that the proposed Chicago Empowerment Zone would be composed of three noncontiguous areas, called _clusters_, rather than a single, concentrated section of the city. These clusters represent the various communities contained within the noncontiguous areas making up the zone. The best-qualified areas of Chicago that were not nominated for Empowerment Zone status by the EZ/EC CC were nominated, although ultimately not federally-designated, as Enterprise Communities (ECs); these Enterprise Communities are also considered clusters. The three Empowerment Zone clusters are the South Cluster, the West Cluster, and the Pilsen/Little Village Cluster; the three Enterprise Community clusters are the Calumet Cluster, the New Englewood Village Cluster, and the West Cluster.

Design of the Study

In the context of the above legislative history and the background of the Chicago application process, we assess both the quality of citizen participation in the feeder application process and its effect on the overall Chicago EZ/EC application. First, however, we must define the term *citizen participation*. The interpretations vary according to one's perspective; for example, President Clinton used the term *grassroots*. The HUD regulations never define citizen participation, but rather provide specific plan elements that characterize it, such as participation by both individuals and groups (community, private, nonprofit, and so on). On the basis of the CBO behavior cited throughout this study, community organizations apparently viewed citizen participation as the involvement of non-government individuals throughout the EZ/EC decision-making process. Another level of citizen participation is that of nonaffiliated individual residents. Often these people are most strongly affected by poverty alleviation legislation, but are hardest to reach in terms of citizen participation. As the process progressed, the city apparently changed its behavior, if not its philosophy, about citizen participation in that instead of simply allowing citizen review of decisions, it participated in joint decision-making with the community.

For the purpose of this study, we examine citizen participation in the context of the HUD regulations. We took a pragmatic approach and designed a study that addresses citizen participation through three specific question areas. For the purposes of this report, these areas are termed *process*, *content*, and *product*.

Process: Was the feeder application community-based? If it was, did it include participation by both residents and CBOs? The intent of the citizen participation initiative is to involve persons affected by poverty as well as organizations providing assistance to those in poverty; thus it is important to determine whether citizen participation in the feeder application process involved nonaffiliated residents as well as CBOs.

Content: Were the activities described in the feeder applications focused on direct services to the residents, or on business incentives? This question is important because the state enterprise zone program has been criticized for failing to provide opportunities for the truly impoverished; instead, it mainly addressed business incentives. One goal of the Federal Empowerment Zone effort is to address this concern; therefore the content question evaluates whether this effort focuses on the truly impoverished.

Product: Did Chicago's application represent the communities' proposals? This question is important because the impact on the final plan is the ultimate test of the effectiveness of citizen participation in the application process.

Methodology

In the process analysis, the evaluation focuses on the six main feeder applications used to create the Chicago Strategic Plan and their compliance with HUD regulations regarding citizen participation. We take this approach because HUD required citizen participation as part of the process; thus their regulations would be the most suitable criteria for assessing this question area. To obtain an overall picture of citizen participation, we examined the "citizen participation" portions of the HUD regulations; reviewed the six applications; examined official documents including the Chicago Strategic Plan and the Memorandum of Agreement involving HUD, the City of Chicago, and the State of Illinois; reviewed the records of two focus groups conducted by the National Empowerment Zone Action Research Project; and conducted structured interviews of involved residents, CBO members, city of Chicago officials, and HUD officials.

In the content analysis we applied very simple criteria. Using the materials we had evaluated in the process analysis, we made a general assessment of each plan to determine whether it included projects that addressed citizens' direct needs and opportunities, as opposed to business needs.

In the final portion of this project, the product analysis, we examined whether the Chicago Strategic Plan incorporated specific efforts outlined in the individual Empowerment Zone and Enterprise Community applications. These applications are the most tangible statement of residents' concerns. Consequently, by assessing whether the City of Chicago's submission to HUD was composed of community-initiated proposals, we learned whether citizen participation influenced the final plan. We simply compared the Chicago Strategic Plan with the community plans to determine which strategic objectives originated in plan proposals.

Analysis: Process and Content

The following analyses of the feeder documents are based on the HUD criteria, the interviews, and the individual plan analyses. Those analyses, in turn, are based on reviews of the individual plans, interview data, focus group data, Volume 2 of Chicago's application, and the Chicago Strategic Plan. Because the data gathering for this study concentrated on tangible items such as meeting times and public notification, we do not consistently attempt, in the discussion below, to address more qualitative issues such as plan philosophy. However, if we encountered any qualitative information that added to any individual plan analysis, we included it in the discussion.

Chicago's Empowerment Zone
The South Side Cluster

The South Side feeder application process created a comprehensive plan using both group and individual citizen participation. The plan mentioned the various groups that collaborated to create the South Side plan: 50 community-based organizations, neighborhood block clubs, churches, other institutions, schools, local school councils, and local advisory councils. Along with individual residents, these groups collaborated to help plan, develop, and write the South Side strategic plan.

The South Side feeder application, however, overlooked a few HUD regulations regarding group participants. The plan did not provide a history of the groups in the community, evidence of participants' diversity, evidence of participants' disagreement, or how disagreements were resolved.

Regarding content, the application included both individual and business-oriented projects and programs, but the plan unmistakably emphasized individual low-income residents. It described the resources and assets of the area that could be used to implement the planned projects and programs, such as vocational training, youth development programs, affordable housing, and more community recreational facilities.

The West Side Cluster

Though the six clusters took slightly different approaches to the Empowerment Zone application process, the West Side area was distinctive. Of the West Side communities that originally applied, only a portion was actually included in the Chicago Empowerment Zone. Many West Side residents felt that the geographic heart of the West Side proposal had been excluded from the Empowerment Zone. After lengthy negotiations among all participants in the process, the Chicago City Council helped to resolve the problem by allowing any disputed areas (also including Englewood and Calumet) to be included in an Enterprise Community application. The Council allowed any EC to receive the same city waivers as the proposed EZ, whether federally designated or not.

Because portions of several West Side communities were in either an EC or an EZ, the West Cluster Empowerment Zone Collaborative (WCEZC) was established. The WCEZC made a commitment to serve as the organizational structure connecting the West Side communities represented in both proposals. Moreover, the WCEZC and all participants in the application process viewed the strategic plans in both applications as a single plan. Therefore, we evaluate the West Side (EZ and EC) area as one cluster.

Both individuals and groups participated in the West Side EZ and EC application processes. Community-based organizations used flyers and mailings to publicize meetings. The strategic plan, the interviews, and the support from the "Our Partners" section of the strategic plan all indicate that individual residents participated in the application process. Most of the participants, however, represented groups, primarily CBOs. Even so, the CBO representatives often were West Side residents as well, and therefore served their community in two ways. Possibly more individual residents would have participated if the meetings had better accommodated working residents' schedules (for example, by meeting in the evening or on weekends).

Although the West Side's plan adhered to HUD's regulations as a whole, its description of the participating groups was limited to a historical account of these groups in the West Side communities that they served and/or represented.

Although they did not ignore business, most of the projects and programs included in the West Side plan targeted individuals. Individually oriented initiatives included job skills training programs, drug abuse prevention programs, recycling programs, affordable housing, college preparation programs, legal and financial aid services, and community policing programs.

The Pilsen/Little Village Cluster

Nonaffiliated residents apparently had little involvement in the Pilsen/Little Village application process. The document generally was the product of two self-selected individuals involved in CBOs with input from focus groups composed of other CBO representatives. The minimal involvement by residents is consistent with the fact that the meetings were usually held at 8:30 in the morning and that meeting announcement flyers were distributed only to CBOs.

The application did not address significant expectations for participant involvement as outlined in the HUD regulations. Selection of participants, the role of participants, and dispute resolution were not discussed.

Despite the business focus of the citizen participation process, Table 5.1 shows that this plan comprehensively addressed most of the goals and objectives found in the Chicago Strategic Plan, from the standpoint of both business and citizens' needs.

Table 5. 1	PROCESS AND CONTENT SUMMARY				
Zone *Location*	Direct Resident Participation	Convenient Meetings Times	Public Notice	Met all Significant HUD Requirements	Resident Oriented Projects
South Cluster EZ	Yes	Yes	Yes	Yes	Yes
West Cluster EZ/EC	Yes	Some	Yes	No	Yes
Pilsen/Little Village EZ	Some	Some	Some	No	Yes
New Englewood Village EC	?*	Yes	Yes	No	Yes
Calumet Communities EC	Yes	Some	Yes	Yes	Yes

*   This plan indicated extensive block club participation, but contained no information suggesting individual involvement.

**   Some = Occassional

Chicago's Enterprise Communities
The New Englewood Village Cluster

Apparently the New Englewood Village collaborative process included no involvement by non-CBOs. The application discussed the activities of a number of CBOs and mentioned the large number of active block clubs, but provided no information on individual residents either in regard to their participation or as names of sponsors in an attachment. Further, the plan stated that its writers were self-selected because of the time commitment needed for development of the plan; this suggests involvement by an exclusive group. The plan itself omitted items that might indicate residents' involvement, such as examples of controversies and information about their resolution.

Overall, it appears that the application process was governed by the Community Alternative Policing Strategy (C.A.P.S.) Group. The flyers announcing meetings were sent to persons on this group's mailing list. Much of the plan centered on crime in the area and on the fact that C.A.P.S. had reduced these problems. Many of the activities centered on community policing.

Regarding content, the application included resident-oriented activities such as community policing, youth intervention programs, and community festivals. Business proposals were limited, perhaps because (according to interviews) there is currently very little business activity in the area.

The Calumet Cluster

Citizen participation apparently was quite comprehensive in the development of the Enterprise Community application from the Calumet Communities Consortium. The local community meetings were held frequently (seven sponsored by the CBOs and eight working meetings) and were accessible to residents; a large number of organizations (35) were involved; residents were included as partners from the development through the writing to the post-designation stages; and the proposed governance approach involved another vehicle for drawing citizens into the effort. This assessment of extensive citizen participation was confirmed both in the focus group notes and in our interviews. Yet the interviews also confirm that despite the outreach effort, only a few non-CBO members participated.

Not only did the documentation indicate substantial citizen participation; in addition, the application itself addressed all the citizen participation areas outlined in the HUD regulations, thus highlighting the community's effort to address the citizen participation concerns of the federal government.

Regarding content, the application included both resident- and business-oriented activities. Examples of direct services proposed for residents included developing job skills training programs, extending funding for dislocated workers, and developing health care delivery programs.

Interview Data

To supplement our reviews of the written material relating to citizen participation, the study team conducted 15 interviews. These interviews present three distinct perspectives—from HUD, the city, and the citizen participants—and thus provide a much richer view of citizen participation in the application process.

The interviews confirmed that the communities and the City of Chicago initially followed separate but parallel tracks in developing plans. The communities started developing plans early in the process because the Community Workshop on Economic Development (CWED) disseminated information before the regulations were issued. This early start made them more sophisticated about their expectations regarding citizen participation. When the city's process began, the city had to alter its original process for plan development to bring the two tracks together.

That change was evident in activities such as the addition of community members to the Coordinating Council and the development of a Strategic Plan writing group with significant community involvement.

Two issues surfaced from the HUD interviews. First, although citizen participation was certainly an important part of the HUD selection process, other issues such as geography were considered as well. Second, HUD apparently did not have a precise definition of citizen participation and expected the applicants to develop innovative approaches. In this case, Chicago's application process was both unique and highly regarded. However, the approach resulted in an application without sufficiently detailed plans and programs. In turn, the lack of detail caused differences in post-application interpretations of plan provisions, such as citizen participation in the implementation of the zone. Also, as the interviews indicate, HUD has no ready answers for these issues and expects the city and the community to work them out.

In addition, the city interviews revealed two issues. First, although the citizen participation process certainly created a new kind of coalition in the community development application process, direct involvement by nonaffiliated residents was limited. The second concern was the impact of partisan politics on the process. A few interviewees suggested that elected community officials or other political activists were quietly involved in the process, probably through their connections to various CBOs. Because of the focus of this study, we did not obtain enough information to explore whether political individuals dominated the process behind the scenes.

The participants interviewed were generally enthusiastic about the application process, possibly because most of them were affiliated with a CBO and because CBO members generally were involved in the process, either directly or through consultation, from the discussion stage to reviewing the finished application. All of our informants felt that the process was representative and that the residents were pleased. A few interviewees, however, commented that some of the participants were not totally satisfied, perhaps because their favorite project was not included or had lost its individual identity in the Strategic Plan.

Summary: Process and Content

In regard to the process of citizen participation, we first reviewed the feeder documents for compliance with the HUD regulations related to citizen participation. Three of these submissions omitted discussions about plan development controversies and how participants were to resolve discussions required by the HUD regulations. Possibly there was little controversy because citizen participation was limited in these cases. In regard to this point, the interviews also raised questions about the openness of the plan development process. For example, some observations suggested that the plan writers were a small group, self-selected according to the amount of time they could invest in the process. In another case, the plan was developed through focus groups of CBO leaders and then was written by two of these individuals.

We found considerable citizen participation by CBOs in the entire EZ/EC undertaking. CBOs learned early about the legislation and began to organize community informational meetings before the city did so. They were appointed to the Coordinating Council; they served on the writing committee; and they influenced the kinds of projects that were included in their local feeder applications and in the Chicago Strategic Plan.

The interviews and our review of the documents show that nonaffiliated residents' participation was limited, even though all of the clusters took steps to notify the public (see Table 5.1). Some communities actively sought resident participants by providing house-to-house notifications. Others apparently concentrated their efforts on CBO flyers and word of mouth. As stated earlier, one group merely emphasized CBO focus groups as the main source of input; this made us question whether some CBOs neglect the need for participation by individual, generally nonaffiliated residents.

Whatever approach was taken, however, the interviews suggest that the result was much the same: limited involvement by unaffiliated residents. Unlike some of the city meetings, all community meetings were held in the immediate area, so location was not a problem. As summarized in Table 5.1, however, meeting times were not always convenient because many were scheduled during typical working hours. Perhaps this point helps to explain the minimal individual involvement, although the communities that regularly held meetings in the evening or on Saturdays did not seem to attract more residents than the others. Another possible explanation is that the residents know their CBOs and trust the CBOs' ability to represent them. Further research would be needed to confirm or dispute this explanation.

Even despite limited resident participation, our review of the EZ/EC applications supports the perception that residents' interests were addressed. As shown in Table 5.1, all of the applications contained resident-oriented projects. But are the resident-oriented projects proposed in a plan fostered by a CBO, even with the recognition that CBO members are also residents, the same types of projects as might be included in a plan developed by nonaffiliated residents? The CBO interviewees universally said that the residents were pleased with the outcome, so presumably the answer to this question is "yes." Further interviews with residents are needed, however, to confirm this view.

The Product

Each of the strategic plans in the six individual EZ/EC feeder applications specifies to some degree the proposals advocated by the community to accomplish its vision. We assume, on the basis of individual interviews, that the six documents represent the consensus reached by citizens during their participation in the individual forums. Accordingly, these documents reflect the outcome of citizen participation in the planning process.

In turn, Chicago's Strategic Plan contains seven strategic initiatives aimed at making the plan's vision a reality. Each initiative is supported by a series of goals, which in turn are supported by objectives and specific proposals. The seven initiatives are as follows:

♦ Linking health and human services
♦ Public safety
♦ Economic empowerment
♦ Development of affordable and accessible housing
♦ Building on cultural diversity as a critical asset
♦ Youth futures
♦ Human and organizational capacity building

In the following section we examine whether the objectives in Chicago's Strategic Plan were influenced by proposals for projects in the strategic plans of the six individual EZ/EC feeder applications. The strategic objectives are the means by which the strategic initiatives are to be carried out. Similarly, the proposals in the six documents express the means by which citizens in the EZ/EC communities want their communities to develop. If citizen participation in the entire planning process had a significant impact, the program and project proposals from the six documents should be reflected in the goals and objectives set forth in Chicago's Strategic Plan.

Linking Health and Human Services

The Strategic Plan incorporates five strategies for linking health and human services. These strategies, which receive substantial support in the individual documents, are as follows:

♦ Establish a continuum of health care spanning a lifetime while emphasizing women and children.
♦ Establish better linkages between health and human service providers.
♦ Reinforce and promote healthy lifestyles and behavior.
♦ Eliminate attitudinal and physical barriers to a variety of services.
♦ Build healthy neighborhood open spaces.

A continuum of care

This strategy essentially was drafted by the New Englewood document, which provides the core of the strategic objectives. New Englewood's proposals include early identification of health problems in children and employer screening programs. The West Side and Calumet documents also supported elements of the strategy, such as providing child care and establishing birthing centers.

Better linkages

Most elements of this strategy come from the feeder documents. The Pilsen/Little Village document suggested two proposals to develop better health care linkages in the community. Calumet also submitted a proposal for better linkage. The New Englewood document contributed the idea of creating a one-stop shop for human support services. The South Side proposed attracting health-related industries through tax breaks and other incentives. However, the documents do not mention a major objective under this strategy, namely facilitating health care for uninsured persons.

Lifestyles, barriers, and open spaces

Only the West Side document addressed the strategy of promoting healthy lifestyles. It offered several proposals for drug prevention programs. However, these issues are also discussed in the public safety strategic initiative of the Strategic Plan. New Englewood, Calumet, and Pilsen/Little Village offered proposals under this strategy to eliminate attitudinal and physical barriers. Calumet suggested a mobile health center to make facilities more accessible; New Englewood and Pilsen/Little Village presented proposals for enhancing cultural sensitivity to address the strategy for eliminating attitudinal barriers. The West Side offered the only proposal for the strategy of building healthy neighborhood open spaces.

The strategies for linking health and human services which are presented in the Chicago Strategic Plan are generally supported by proposals found in the feeder applications.

Public Safety

The individual documents address public safety issues to varying degrees. New Englewood presented a detailed plan, but the issue was not included at all in the South Side document. Chicago's Strategic Plan reflects a consensus in the documents that addressed public safety. The Strategic Plan presents two strategies in this area:

♦ Increase the responsibility of residents in community policing.
♦ Increase community policing.

Increased responsibility of residents in community policing

The two objectives for increasing residents' responsibility in community policing are to include community participation in local policing and to train local residents in conflict resolution.

Although the South Side document did not address public safety issues, each of the other feeder documents stressed the need for the entire community to become involved in community policing. Again, the various documents differed in the extent to which they offered specific proposals. New Englewood offered an extensive plan to involve the community in public safety concerns. These proposals support the strategy's intention to increase the responsibility of the community.

Although Pilsen/Little Village offered only one proposal for increasing public safety, this was one of the few specific programs mentioned in the Strategic Plan. The Safe Paths program, proposed by the Latino Youth organization, attempts to provide safe passage for children to and from school by enlisting senior citizens and other residents as monitors. New Englewood also mentioned a Safe Path program for students. The Strategic Plan specifically mentioned this proposal as a method of increasing community participation in local policing. Another detailed approach proposed by the Strategic Plan is the creation of block clubs and park advisory councils. Block clubs received strong support in Calumet and New Englewood.

The Strategic Plan calls for training local residents in conflict resolution. This was not mentioned in the available documents, but can be viewed as a natural extension of the strategy to increase residents' responsibility.

Increased community policing

As stated above, the second public safety strategy calls for increased community policing. New Englewood and the West Side expressed strong support for the Community Alternative Policing Strategy (C.A.P.S.) and wanted to expand the program into targeted communities. Calumet endorsed a collaborative relationship between community residents and the police. However, it is unclear whether Calumet endorsed the C.A.P.S. program.

As mentioned earlier, the information available from the individual documents shows considerable support for the strategies and objectives proposed in the public safety initiative.

Economic Empowerment

The economic empowerment initiative consists of six strategies:
- ♦ Promote financial development.
- ♦ Promote neighborhood enterprise development.
- ♦ Provide job development and access strategies.
- ♦ Provide land and capital improvements.
- ♦ Promote education and training.
- ♦ Provide programmatic and personal capacities strategies.

Financial development

The financial development strategy contains nine objectives that include a wide range of interests such as facilitating capital availability to EZ/EC businesses, developing industrial corridors, and developing international trade relations. Most of these objectives were supported by clear references in the six individual documents.

Facilitation of loans for small businesses and micro-enterprises was supported by the South Side, Calumet, and New Englewood documents. The South Side called for subsidized and guaranteed loan programs for both micro-enterprises and small businesses. New Englewood addressed the need for start-up and operating funds for businesses.

Development of industrial corridors and industrial parks was supported by proposals from Calumet and Pilsen/Little Village, which called for industrial corridors at specific locations in their areas. New Englewood and Calumet supported the proposal to develop and promote international trade relations. The New Englewood document proposed the creation of a free trade zone as a means of establishing ties to the North American Free Trade Agreement (NAFTA). Calumet's proposal to expand funding for business training initiatives was expressed in the objective of developing incentives for large businesses that train and hire EZ/EC residents. The objective of stimulating self-investment in the EZ/EC areas was supported by New Englewood's proposal to establish supportive mechanisms such as credit unions, cooperative banks/community finance corporations, and local endowment funds.

A proposal by New Englewood may have formed the basis for the objective of structuring ongoing cooperative businesses that the community can own and operate. Otherwise the feeder documents did not seem to refer directly to this objective. The objective of establishing a revolving loan fund may or may not be a generalization of Pilsen/Little Village's proposal to create a grant and loan pool for business incubators. The final strategic objective, attracting private investment, apparently did not come from the six documents. However, it is so general that it might be considered an integral part of the financing proposals discussed earlier.

Neighborhood enterprise development

The neighborhood enterprise development strategy has two strategic objectives: to support existing resident-owned businesses, and to create alternative credit resources to finance existing businesses and new entrepreneurs that historically have been denied access to capital.

The first objective was supported by numerous proposals in the documents, including the following: Calumet proposed an import substitution study to increase local supply of inputs, and also proposed to expand existing business retention programs. Pilsen/Little Village wanted to provide management and financial assistance to businesses. New Englewood wished to increase market trade by using the unique cultural assets of the community.

Job development and access strategies

The job development and access strategy contains ten objectives. The South Side provided some support for the objective of creating jobs in allied health fields, tourism, and other industries by using financial incentives. The South Side, New Englewood, and Pilsen/Little Village supported the objective of developing employment partnerships with new businesses. The objective of training residents for the new jobs was supported by West Side and Calumet documents.

New Englewood's proposal to connect residents to regional employment opportunities formed the basis for the strategic objective of expanding regional access to jobs. The South Side document provided the foundation for the objective of expanding the "McLaughlin Ordinance," which stipulates that Chicagoans work one-half of their employment hours on city-sponsored construction projects. Two objectives called for the creation of a database for job seekers and job openings; the South Side and Pilsen/Little Village documents supported these objectives.

The objective of developing hiring agreements with labor unions working on projects in or near the zone may have originated in the New Englewood document.

Two other objectives, however, apparently did not originate in the six documents: (1) committing to infrastructure upgrades to facilitate attraction of businesses and (2) attracting businesses that are committed to the development of the community.

Land and capital improvement

The objective of improving public safety to attract business received support in several documents. The section in this report concerning the Strategic Plan's public safety initiative deals with public safety concerns; the five remaining objectives were not addressed directly in the documents. Pilsen/Little Village's proposal to clean up contaminated industrial sites could be viewed as support for the objective of improving the investment climate in the zone or establishing an attractive physical environment for economic investment. None of the six documents, however, gave any evidence of generating the following three objectives:

♦ Create a barrier-free zone for people with disabilities.

♦ Create opportunities for zone residents and businesses to improve the physical environment.

♦ Develop a land trust strategy that is acceptable to the community and compatible with the political process.

Education and training

The four strategic objectives for this strategy are (1) to prepare residents for existing and future jobs, (2) to develop business and school interchange in the development of training curriculums, (3) to create educational and training programs that motivate the participants, and (4) to assist residents in identifying personal and career development strategies.

The documents strongly supported the first objective, preparing residents for existing and future jobs. New Englewood offered a number of proposals for youth-operated businesses that will prepare young residents for the labor force. The Calumet document made two proposals in support of the second objective, developing an interchange between businesses and schools. The two remaining objectives are also found in the Strategic Initiative on Human and Organizational Capacity Building. Support for these two objectives was expressed in New Englewood's proposal to supplement on-the-job training with a pre-employment core curriculum stressing areas such as grooming, business behavior, and goal setting.

Programmatic and personal capacities

The strategy to increase programmatic and personal capacities has three strategic objectives: (1) to increase capabilities for local economic leadership; (2) to assure that job training is linked to viable economic opportunity; and (3) to assure that Zone-based support services are in place to facilitate economic development.

We found support for the first objective in a number of documents. As stated above, Pilsen/Little Village wished to provide management and financial assistance to businesses. This objective was also supported by the above-mentioned proposals to assist micro-enterprises and small business. The West Side stated that the residents' capacity to succeed in self-employment and micro-enterprise development could be encouraged with assistance from established organizations. The final two objectives were not mentioned directly but were supported indirectly in the documents.

Most of these objectives were supported by proposals from the feeder documents. The significant objectives that do not appear to come from the documents concern physical improvements and land banking.

Development of Affordable and Accessible Housing

The Strategic Plan contains four strategies for development of affordable and accessible housing:
- Develop supportive housing programs and delivery systems.
- Increase housing development capacity.
- Preserve and rehabilitate affordable and accessible housing.
- Provide transitional housing.

These strategies were reflected to various degrees in the individual documents.

Supportive housing programs and delivery systems

The Strategic Plan proposed the following objectives to provide supportive housing programs and delivery systems. The first objective is to coordinate the activities of the Chicago Housing Authority with an overall plan for developing accessible and affordable community housing. This proposal was not found in any of the documents. The documents, however, gave widespread support to the second objective, expansion of home ownership opportunities. The third objective was to provide vouchers based on Section 8 projects to alleviate overcrowded and substandard housing. The West Side and Pilsen/Little Village documents both incorporated the use of rental certificates or vouchers, but they emphasized Chicago Housing Authority residents and very low-income residents who previously had been denied certificates rather than alleviation of overcrowded and substandard housing.

The fourth objective was to increase and facilitate housing for low-income senior citizens. The West Side and New Englewood documents offered proposals for the construction of new senior housing, funding for housing rehabilitation, and a volunteer program to repair and maintain housing owned by seniors and the disabled. The fifth objective was to promote residents' control of public housing. The South Side and Calumet documents supported resident management programs that would lead to residents' ownership of public housing units. The final objective was to increase housing accessibility for the disabled. New Englewood was the only document that addressed this objective; it concentrated on the repair program cited above.

Housing development capacity

The objectives for increasing housing development capacity emphasize that local community development organizations purchase and rehabilitate housing units before selling them on terms favorable to owners or occupants. The West Side and Pilsen/Little Village documents supported this strategy.

Preservation and rehabilitation of affordable and accessible housing

This strategy emphasizes historic preservation and the special requirements for preserving historic buildings. The documents expressed a great deal of support for rehabilitating buildings but did not mention historic preservation in connection with housing. Rather, historic preservation was mentioned in connection with establishing a tourist culture based on the historical significance of certain areas.

Special needs and transitional housing strategies

The final strategy targets special needs and transitional housing. We found moderate support in the documents for the West Side and Pilsen/Little Village proposals for seniors and the disabled. The West Side also proposed plans for young adult housing services. However, we found no provisions for recovering drug users, group homes, or AIDS patients, such as exist in the Strategic Plan.

Except for the objectives providing for historic preservation and transitional housing, the housing proposals in the Chicago Strategic Plan received considerable support in the individual documents.

Building on Cultural Diversity as a Critical Asset

The Strategic Plan lists three strategies to build on cultural diversity in the EZ/EC areas:

♦ Increase and promote cultural sensitivity;

♦ Increase recreational opportunities.

♦ Promote tourism development strategies.

Cultural sensitivity and recreational opportunities

These strategies rely on cultural activities, such as painting murals, which further social service goals. The plan urges increased recreational opportunities to decrease gang activities. Tourism development strategies are advocated to stimulate economic activity by developing an area's cultural assets and heritage.

Support for these strategies was found in the West Side, New Englewood, and Pilsen/Little Village documents. The West Side listed rather broad proposals as support for increasing cultural sensitivity through cultural activities. New Englewood proposed using community festivals as a means of expressing cultural diversity.

Tourism development strategies

The New Englewood document emphasized the promotion of culturally based businesses. These proposals included marketing the area's culture, marketing cultural assets to increase trade, and establishing relationships with Asian businesses. Much of the Pilsen/Little Village's strategic plan used cultural assets for promoting tourism and local businesses; that document listed six specific proposals for this purpose, including establishing a tourism center, a cultural center, and a culturally based retail incubator.

Most of the strategies and objectives in this strategic initiative were supported by the individual documents. As stated earlier, the proposal to increase recreational opportunities did not originate in the discussions of cultural diversity found in the documents. The overall strategy of promoting cultural sensitivity was expressed in documents from the West Side and Pilsen Little Village. New Englewood and Pilsen/Little Village proposed to develop cultural assets for economic gain in the community.

Youth Futures

The Chicago Strategic Plan offers three strategies for enhancing the future of young people living in EZ/EC areas. These were supported in the individual documents:

♦ Provide youth-run businesses, youth training, and youth education.
♦ Increase youth intervention and mentoring.
♦ Develop lighted schoolhouses.

Youth-run businesses, training, and education.

The individual documents suggested a wide range of youth-oriented business, training, and education programs. Pilsen/Little Village stated that community institutions and organizations would play an important part in providing opportunities to resident youths. That document, however, proposed only one objective: that the Junior Achievement Program be introduced into area schools. The West Side did not present a plan for enhancing youth employment training, but it recommended that a shuttle service be established to carry local youths to suburban jobs. The Calumet plan advocated a range of unspecified work-experience programs for area youths that would facilitate the transition from school to work.

The South Side plan targeted at-risk youths through comprehensive employment training in schools; the job-training programs would be modeled after the Youth Build Program. The South Side plan also proposed the establishment of programs to involve local youths in business training and micro-enterprises.

New Englewood offered a detailed, comprehensive plan for youth opportunities, involving a variety of training and education programs. These included early-age entrepreneurship training, apprenticeship opportunities, and a school-to-work program. The plan also called for enrolling high school dropouts in a combined GED/job training program. Some of the proposals for youth-run businesses included youth incubator projects and a youth-operated Habitat for Humanity program.

Youth intervention and mentoring

The second strategy proposes youth intervention and mentoring. Each of the feeder documents supported mentoring programs. Youth development agencies at local schools were the suggested avenues. The South Side and West Side documents stressed the need for programs aimed at preventing substance abuse.

The New Englewood plan offered the most detailed proposals for youth intervention and monitoring. Its proposals for targeting at-risk students included expanding Head Start Programs, providing after-school tutoring, peer counseling and mentoring, and gang intervention.

Lighted schoolhouses

This strategy is intended to use schoolhouses more fully for extended education and other community programs. The West Side, Calumet, and New Englewood plans expressed support for using area educational institutions in this way. Pilsen/Little Village proposed a Community-Based Educational Opportunity Center enabling residents to acquire the skills and information needed to pursue higher education.

As stated above, the strategies found in this initiative were supported by proposals from the feeder documents.

Human and Organizational Capacity Building

The Chicago Strategic Plan states that personal and community empowerment can be achieved only after developing skills and resources. The two strategies in this initiative are designed to enable individuals and communities to become empowered:

♦ Build programmatic and personal capacities.

♦ Expand job training and adult education opportunities.

The Strategic Plan proposes several objectives to achieve these two strategies; these objectives incorporate many found in other initiatives. Because they are fairly broad, we easily found them supported in the individual documents.

Programmatic and personal capacities

Typical objectives supported in the feeder documents were to develop individual and organizational capacities for economic development; to develop interpersonal skills and sharing, which encourage lifelong holistic community revitalization; to foster a sense of family self-sufficiency; to give residents tools to train themselves to accept more responsibility and work to remove themselves from poverty; and to encourage a culturally based educational and social training curriculum.

Job training and adult education opportunities

The Pilsen/Little Village document proposed several projects that met the criteria for these objectives. That community's proposals for a computer lab and a family literacy program met three of the objectives.

The other documents strongly supported the objectives set forth in this initiative. The South Side document recognized the connection between enhanced education and personal capacity, employment training, and job opportunities. It also offered proposals for targeting at-risk youths and building personal capacity. The New Englewood document offered an extensive plan including apprenticeship programs, school-to-work programs, and workforce preparation for young people and adults. That plan also proposed to educate residents about their obligations and opportunities as citizens. The lighted schoolhouse proposal, for example, discussed above, would facilitate adult education and community development. The West Side offered a series of proposals to increase human and organizational capacity, such as establishing connections with local schools, hospitals, and other institutions to develop leadership skills and capacity building. The West Side document also focused on increasing residents' job readiness.

Although all of the objectives in this initiative were supported in the individual documents, the Strategic Plan emphasizes opportunities for veterans and the disabled, which are not stressed in those documents.

Governance

Another key product of citizen participation, although not a strategic initiative, is governance. We regard the governance proposals as crucial in developing plans in the Chicago EZ/EC process. The Chicago Strategic

Plan includes a governance proposal; such proposals are intrinsic to three of the feeder applications. A permanent Coordinating Council was discussed in the South Side, New Englewood, and Calumet documents. The Council would serve as a legitimate decision-making body. Suggestions for representation on the Council varied: The South Side and Calumet members were to be elected, and the New Englewood members were to be appointed by the mayor.

Membership on the Council is viewed as a way to include impoverished and working-class residents as well as CBO representatives in the bottom-up implementation process and to achieve HUD's goals as well as the communities' principle of alleviating poverty.

Product Summary

Table 5.2 summarizes the results of the product analysis. Because the West Side EZ and EC applications contained essentially the same proposals, they are combined into one column. Overall, the table shows that most of the strategic initiatives initially were supported by all of the applying communities. The one exception involves the South EZ which did not include public safety or cultural diversity initiatives in its application.

Table 5.2	**APPLICATION SOURCE OF CHICAGO STRATEGIC PLAN OBJECTIVES**					
Initiatives and Objectives	South EZ	West EZ/EC	Pilsen EZ	New Engl. EC	Cal. EC	None
Linking Health Care and Human Services						
Continuum of Care		X		X	X	
Build Better Linkages	X		X		X	X
Promote Healthy Lifestyles		X				
Eliminate Barriers			X	X	X	
Healthy Neighborhoods		X				
Public Safety						
Increased Resident Resp.		X	X	X	X	
Increased Com. Policing		X		X	X	
Economic Empowerment						
Financial Development	X		X	X	X	
Neighborhood Enterprise			X	X	X	
Job Development	X	X	X	X	X	X
Land & Capital Improvement			X			X
Education and Training				X	X	
Personal Capacity Strategies		X	X			

Initiatives and Objectives	South EZ	West EZ/EC	Pilsen EZ	New Engl. EC	Cal. EC	None
Development of Affordable and Accessible Housing						
Supportive Housing Prog.	X	X	X	X	X	X
Housing Develop. Capacity		X	X			
Housing Rehabilitation	X	X	X	X	X	
Special Needs and Transitional		X	X			X
Building on Cultural Diversity as a Critical Asset						
Increase Cultural Sensitivity	X	X	X	X	X	
Increase Recreation Opport.	X	X	X	X	X	
Promote Tourism		X	X	X	X	
Youth Futures						
Youth-Run Businesses	X	X	X	X	X	
Youth Intervention	X	X	X	X	X	
Lighted Schoolhouses		X	X	X	X	
Human and Organizational Capacity Building						
Build Personal Capacities	X	X	X	X		
Expand Job Training	X	X	X	X	X	

The table also shows that all objectives received support from multiple sources, with three exceptions: promotion of healthy lifestyles, healthy neighborhoods, and increased recreational opportunities.

Table 5.2 reveals that most of the proposals supporting the objectives came from the original community applications and that six objectives generated proposals from all offices that applied: job development, supportive housing programs, housing rehabilitation, youth-run busi-nesses, youth intervention, and expanded job training. Pilsen/Little Village's plan addressed the greatest number of strategic objectives; the South Side plan addressed the fewest.

Overall, the Chicago Strategic Plan reflects the two underlying goals of reinventing government and alleviating poverty. In addition, the strategies and objectives are guided by HUD's four principles (economic opportunity, sustainable community development, community-based partnerships, and strategic vision), which are designed to encourage long-term community development through a bottom-up decision-making process.

The two goals of alleviating poverty and reinventing government were also reflected in the spirit of the six feeder documents. In addition, the proposals in the documents were designed according to the four guiding principles. This analysis of the plans is supported by the comments of several interviewees, who indicated the importance of HUD's principles during community deliberations.

The philosophies of the feeder documents and of the Chicago Strategic Plan are similar because they all rely on the same principles. Yet because the strategic objectives were written so broadly, it is difficult to determine whether any vested interests offered competing strategies. The broad language of the strategic objectives also makes it difficult to determine which specific proposals were included in the Strategic Plan and whether any trends were present in the types of proposals included or not included in the plan.

The proposals designed to improve infrastructure, which do not seem to originate in the individual documents, give the impression that the City proposed its own ideas. As stated earlier, however, the great majority of strategic objectives appear to be based on the individual documents. This implies that the Chicago Strategic Plan in fact was the product of a bottom-up decision-making process.

Findings

Although the strategic objectives are general, they are supported by the specific project proposals found in the six feeder documents. It appears that the citizen participation in the EZ/EC planning process had a significant influence on framing the strategic objectives proposed in the Chicago Strategic Plan.

Because the strategic objectives are so general, it is difficult to determine how each EZ/EC feeder document influenced the Strategic Plan. Possibly some EZ/ECs had greater influence than others, but that information cannot be determined by examining the documents and the Strategic Plan.

The CBOs were the prime movers in citizens' participation in applying for Empowerment Zone status. The CBOs began to learn about the legislation even before the regulations were issued. They organized the community activity and spread the word. CBOs were appointed to the

Coordinating Council by the mayor, and were involved in the process through the writing phase of the application process.

Some EZ/EC applications emphasized interests of the major local CBO. The New Englewood Village Collaborative, for example, which began its information-disseminating process by using the mailing lists for the community policing program, included a significant level of community policing programs in its plan.

The Chicago Strategic Plan is general in part because the complicated citizen participation process consumed much of the application time. Chicago's application is not specific in defining budget, strategic objectives, and implementation projects. The Chicago process—which involved the submission of area proposals to a Coordinating Council, consensus decision making, and a writing committee involved with CBOs—was open but time-consuming. Time was too short to negotiate details; thus only a general plan could be developed.

Residents, particularly those not affiliated with CBOs, had only limited involvement in the application process. Interview data showed that although a few areas, notably the West Side and Calumet, attempted to involve residents, the residents overall were a small presence in the community efforts, possibly because most of the meetings were not convenient for working people. This finding also could mean that the residents were satisfied to be represented by the CBOs. Alternatively, it could mean that the CBOs had neither the resources nor the time to draw residents more fully into the process.

Business as well as community interests are addressed in both the individual documents and the Strategic Plan. Neither interest appears to be predominant, nor do they appear to be coordinated with each other.

Although business incentives and tax breaks are a crucial part of the Empowerment Zone legislation, HUD did not necessarily expect businesses to play a major role in strategic plan development. Many of the depressed areas eligible for Empowerment Zone designation suffer from severe business disinvestment; as a result, few local residents with business skills are available to assist in plan development. Therefore the study team chose not to seek out information on the issue of business participation in plan development. However, we discuss business-related proposals under the "Product" section because these proposals are part of the strategic plans. Also, in the "Process and Content" section, we refer to the absence of business participants in the feeder application process because that issue was raised by some of the interviewees.

Generally, participants had a common definition of "alleviating poverty." This finding is particularly helpful because a primary goal of the empowerment effort is to alleviate poverty.

Generally, the community participants and the public officials had different definitions of "reinventing government." This finding is less helpful because it suggests that the community and the public officials might have different expectations of the citizen participation process, which might cause friction between the parties. According to our interviews, for example, it appears that the city may define "reinventing government" in the post-application process as providing new services to the communities, while the communities may define "reinventing government" as the communities' choosing the new services with little involvement by the city.

Problems Encountered in the Study

We had considerable difficulty in obtaining source documents. For example, we obtained the Enterprise Community plans rather quickly from city officials, but these documents were the final submissions to HUD rather than the material initially submitted to the city. Consequently our product analysis was limited to the content of the final EC submissions which may be somewhat different from the initial community plans for those areas. Certainly it is valuable to determine the relationship between the initiatives in the narrower Enterprise Communities documents and those in the Empowerment Zone plan, which has citywide impact. Ideally, however, the analysis would have involved a comparison between the initial community contributions and the material endorsed by the city.

We encountered similar difficulty in obtaining the Empowerment Zone submissions. In the case of the Empowerment Zone clusters, however, the documents we used clearly predated any decisions by the city. Thus we were better able to trace the inclusion or exclusion of particular elements.

Problems also arose in the interview process. Specifically, the interviews occurred at a time of considerable controversy between the city and the community about citizen participation in the governance process. This controversy had two effects on some interviews: Interviewees found it difficult to differentiate between application citizen participation and governance citizen participation, and interviewees were reluctant to provide information because they questioned the motives behind the interviews.

Because of time constraints, the number of interviews was limited; thus it was it difficult to generalize from the findings. Even so, the interviews were useful in our assessment because the findings were generally consistent, although the sources were varied: CBO members from all areas, city officials, and HUD officials.

No information was available to enable us to identify the source of the cluster proposals or the extent of support for the proposals in the community. Consequently we could not determine whether proposals in the documents represented open community deliberations or some other situation such as long-held vested interests of established groups.

Citizen participation in the application process was one of HUD's requirements for EZ/EC designation. Because of this requirement, local officials may have allowed citizens to participate more fully than usual. Citizens' input may be less extensive or less influential if federal regulations do not explicitly require their participation; this precondition may limit our ability to generalize from our findings.

We cannot address the question of CBO versus direct resident participation and the impact of each because the study was not designed to gather data on that subject. Consequently, although the study found significant citizen participation, this result does not imply *full* citizen participation because the effect of nonaffiliated residents' participation cannot be determined from the data we gathered.

Finally, the study team may have brought biases to the project. One team member lives in one of the areas under study, had been actively involved in the application process, and could have introduced a pro-community bias. Another member is a government employee and could have introduced a pro-government bias. Yet it is also possible that these two perspectives offset each other and brought a better balance to the study.

Points for Future Analysis

This study of citizen participation in the Empowerment Zone/ Enterprise Community application process leaves much room for further research. For example, if the remaining source documents could be obtained, researchers could conduct the "product" portion of this study again to verify its findings.

Also, who created and wrote the strategic proposals that did not originate in the individual documents? Were they created by the combined efforts of the writing group, or did the city bring these plans to the table? In the same vein, some of the strategic objectives are so broad that they may not have been taken from the proposals. The proposals may only appear to have influenced those objectives.

The broad language of the strategic objectives may present problems during implementation of the Strategic Plan. Residents of areas receiving EZ/EC status may expect their specific proposals to be implemented because they fall within the general outline of the Strategic Plan. Yet the Strategic Plan is noncommittal in allocating funds to specific projects; therefore projects which are entirely different from those mentioned in the local documents, but which meet the broad criteria stated in the objectives, may have an equal claim. Problems resulting from implementation of the broad objectives could be a fruitful source of research.

Further research questions surround the issue of resident participation. Why, for example, was participation by nonaffiliated residents limited? If it is assumed that these residents know their own needs best (and that view, in fact, was expressed in the interviews), how do they become involved? Did they stay away because they are confident that the CBOs can represent them best? Did residents play a significant but not readily apparent role in developing the local plan proposals? Extensive interviewing of these individuals could provide some answers.

The limited involvement by business (mostly banks) noted in some of the interviews creates some concern, particularly because business knowledge is crucial to successful economic development. It would be helpful to know why businesses did not participate more fully. Were they uninterested in the effort, or perhaps unaware? It would be useful to explore approaches to increasing the involvement by business so that community and business needs could be met jointly.

In this study, we did not address the involvement of political actors or issues in grassroots citizen participation, although some of the interviews and documents suggested that partisan politics played a part in the EZ/EC process. To learn more about the dynamics of the application process, and whether political activities were part of the process, interviews with community political leaders would be an appropriate area of inquiry.

This analysis of citizen participation in the application process could benefit from a follow-up study of citizen participation in governance and in implementation. It would be interesting to learn whether governance is affected by concerns from the development phase, such as minimal participation by residents, broadly written strategic objectives, and differences in definitions of "reinventing government."

Overall we found that the interviews were a rich source of information which added considerable texture to the overall study. However, the number of interviews was limited by time constraints; also, the interviews generally involved CBO or government officials, who are readily available. Conducting additional interviews and focus groups, particularly among community participants, would help to confirm or refute the findings of this study as well as answer some of the questions we raised above. The interviews in this study tended to include the most active participants in the process; less active individuals might introduce a different perspective.

Conclusions and Predictions

Overall we found that citizen participation in the Chicago EZ/EC application process differed substantially from that in application efforts for previous programs, according to the HUD interviewees. The communities were mobilized from within, and Chicago's application effort surpassed the expectations outlined in the regulations and held by the HUD officials. The proposals from the communities provided the basis for the Chicago Strategic Plan, and the proposals in the plan addressed issues concerning residents' needs.

It is also clear that individual residents' participation was limited. Depending on one's perspective, this situation may or may not be problematic. If one can assume that CBOs understand the residents' concerns and choices, it is not a problem because CBOs governed the process. However, if CBOs failed to comprehend and address residents' concerns and choices, concerning the ultimate goal of citizen participation, the effort was flawed. Only further study can reveal whether individual residents' true concerns were addressed.

On the basis of the information obtained in this study, we offer the following predictions:

♦ Because the Chicago Strategic Plan is so general, because HUD officials are reluctant to assume the role of referee, and because the CBOs have succeeded in taking control of the application process, the

CBOs will continue to negotiate for a community role in the implementation portion of the EZ/EC process.

◆ Because of the serious need for infrastructure improvement in the zone communities and because of the effect of infrastructure on the quality of residents' lives, a significant portion of the zone resources will go to rehabilitation of housing, public transportation, and parklands.

◆ Because of the severe depression in the area and the emphasis of the legislation on citizens' welfare, a significant portion of the resources will be used for social services.

◆ Because of the impact of the CBOs on the plan development process, existing CBO programs will receive increased funding.

Chapter 6

Business and Economic Development in Chicago's Empowerment Zone

John F. McDonald

I n December 1994, the U.S. Department of Housing and Urban Development (HUD) announced that federal Empowerment Zone status had been awarded to six cities, including Chicago. Empowerment Zones are economically depressed areas with a population of no more than 200,000, which meet certain criteria established by HUD in accordance with the enabling federal law. All six Empowerment Zones are relatively small areas within a large metropolitan region. The Chicago Empowerment Zone covers about 14 square miles and has a population of 200,000 (in a metropolitan area of 7 million people).

In this essay, we examine the likely economic effects of the Empowerment Zone program in light of some basic economic and social goals. After briefly describing the incentives for business provided by the program, we consider the fundamental economic and social objectives to which the program might contribute. We conclude that the Empowerment Zone program has the potential to improve both efficiency in using labor resources and equity in distributing the fruits of economic progress.

Next we assess in greater detail the possible economic effects of the program, beginning with a review of a study of the Illinois Enterprise Zone program in Cook County, which was conducted by the author (McDonald 1993). This is followed by a short inventory of the labor force that lives in the Empowerment Zone and existing employment. This inventory reveals that the resident labor force lacks basic educational credentials and has low levels of employment and earnings, but that the employment trends in the area are far from bleak. The Empowerment Zone has an employment base on which it should be possible to build. This economic inventory is followed by a brief look at a recent employment forecast for the nation for 1994-2005, issued by the U.S. Department of Labor. The forecast indicates clearly that much of the employment growth over that decade will be in the service sector, but that some opportunities will exist in other sectors as well. Finally, we draw some conclusions about the economic prospects for the Empowerment Zone.

Empowerment Zone Incentives for Business

The Empowerment Zone program has three features that directly benefit firms located in the Zone. First, through 2001, employers may claim a 20 percent tax credit on the first $15,000 in wages of each employee who lives in the Zone, up to a maximum of $3,000 per employee. The tax credit will be phased out through 2004. Second, a firm in the Zone can claim accelerated depreciation on equipment purchases up to $200,000. The firm can deduct as much as $17,500 more in depreciation than it could claim otherwise, until the total basis of the asset has been claimed. Third, the program creates a new category of tax-exempt municipal bonds called "Qualified Empowerment Zone Facility Bonds," which can be issued on behalf of private firms to finance real estate purchases in the Zone.

The two latter incentives, however, are available only to a special category of businesses located in the Empowerment Zone. These businesses must meet several criteria; potentially the most restrictive is that 35 percent of the employees who work at the establishment in the Empowerment Zone also must be residents of the Zone. This restriction may have little effect on the ability of small businesses serving the local area to participate in the program, but larger enterprises (such as manufacturers that serve the national market) are very unlikely to meet the employee residency criterion. This suggests that the wage tax credit will be the most frequently used business incentive. The wage tax credit is set up particularly to encourage the hiring of workers who earn $15,000 per year or less. For example, suppose that an employer hires four Zone workers at salaries of $15,000 each, or a total wage bill of $60,000. The wage tax credit will be $12,000. If the employer instead hires six Zone workers at salaries of $10,000 each, the wage tax credit is still $12,000. However, if the employer hires three Zone workers at salaries of $20,000 each, the wage tax credit is reduced to $9,000 (and falls to $6,000 if two workers are hired at $30,000 each).

The Empowerment Zone program also includes $100 million in direct federal funding over a period of 10 years for a variety of social programs for residents of the Zone. Community residents and municipal officials are expected to cooperate in planning the use of these funds; other contributors to this book examine this topic in depth.

The incentives for businesses in the Empowerment Zone thus encourage both investment in the Zone and the expansion of employment of Zone residents. In this essay we discuss whether these incentives are likely to produce results that are consistent with society's basic economic goals and objectives.

Goals of Local Economic Development Programs

The first task in formulating a policy for local economic development is to think carefully about the goals that the community wishes to pursue. In the usual statements made by state and local public officials (among others), these goals basically consist of three things: jobs, jobs, and jobs. (Local public officials also wish to expand the local tax base in order to provide better public services and/or impose lower taxes. This goal is worthwhile for the central city, but we do not consider it further here.) There may be nothing wrong with naming jobs as the primary goal, but what is the logic that supports it? For whom are these jobs being created? What about efficient use of resources, equitable distribution of income, and personal freedom? The discipline of economics provides a coherent framework in which to formulate the goals for local economic development policy.

One basic economic goal is the efficient use of resources. When resources are used inefficiently, someone is needlessly worse off because resources have not be put to their best use. In an efficient allocation of resources, it is not possible to increase one person's economic well-being without reducing another's. The goal of policy is to move toward efficient use of resources by identifying policies that indeed increase some people's economic well-being without reducing anyone else's. In the language of cost-benefit analysis, the value of benefits exceeds the value of the costs, and those on whom costs are imposed receive compensation or side payments so as to restore their original levels of well-being.

In practice, however, it is often impossible to fully compensate those on whom costs are imposed. If the value of a policy's benefits exceeds the costs, but if compensation is not paid to keep everyone at or above their initial level of economic well-being, the policy or project in question is said to offer a *potential* improvement in the allocation of resources. The use of this "potential improvement" criterion can be dangerous; for example, it would signal approval of a project that taxes the poor to provide some large benefit for the rich.

Mainstream economists also recognize that an efficient economy can produce a highly unequal distribution of income, and they favor public policies to reduce income inequality. Society may wish to alter the distribution of income through a variety of policy measures, and these measures may reduce the efficiency with which the economy operates. Society also may be willing to tolerate some inefficiency in order to achieve a more equitable distribution of income. The goal of equity in distributing the fruits of the economy, however, is conceptually separate from the goal of efficient allocation of resources.

Consider the goal of equity in more detail. To establish equity as a goal, we must decide on a way to consider the well-being of the members of society together as a whole. We need to know whether the society is better off if we reduce Person A's well-being as we increase Person B's. To address this question, economists recommend the use of a concept known as the *social welfare function*, which expresses the economic well-being of the entire society as it depends on the well-being of each member. Most economists, and most other people as well, think that society's well-being is increased if anyone in that society becomes better off. They also believe, however, that an increase in a poor person's well-being will increase social welfare more than an equal increase in that of a rich person. In other words, they think a redistribution of income from a rich person to a poor person increases social welfare.

A controversial special case of a social welfare function was proposed by moral philosopher John Rawls (1971), who argued that social welfare is not improved unless the economic well-being of the person with the lowest level is increased. How does Rawls justify such a function for social welfare? He thinks that the members of society would agree on this function in what he calls the "original position." The original position refers to the hypothetical time when people come together to make up the rules for a society without specific knowledge of their positions within that society. They do not know whether they will be rich or poor, intelligent or dull. Rawls thinks the rational person would not agree "in advance" to a social welfare function that would permit society to reduce his or her well-being to enhance someone else's. Instead Rawls thinks that the rational person adopts what is called the "maximin" rule, which ranks alternatives by their worst outcomes. This is a rule for pessimists, those who assume that the worst is likely to happen.

Few mainstream economists advocate the use of the Rawlsian social welfare function because they think that people are not such pessimists. Yet, one of the most thoughtful practitioners of local economic development, the late Robert Mier, wrote a book entitled *Social Justice and Local Development Policy* (1993), in which he adopted the Rawls viewpoint. As Commissioner of Economic Development for the City of Chicago in the 1980s, Mier tried consistently to favor policies and processes for policy formulation that tended to increase the well-being of those who had the least. In his book he recounts his experiences as a public official in the administration of Mayor Harold Washington.

How do the likely economic effects of the Empowerment Zone program measure up against the goals of equity and efficient use of resources? Recall that the Empowerment Zone program includes financial incentives for (selected) businesses to locate in the Zone (accelerated depreciation and low-interest loans) and, once they have located there, to hire workers who live in the Zone (wage tax credit). Also, any business located in the Zone is eligible for the wage tax credit and potentially eligible for the other incentives. A reduction in labor costs may enable existing businesses to grow. If these incentives work as expected, more jobs and more real property will be located in the Zone, and more Zone residents will be employed than without the program. The Empowerment Zone, however, covers only a rather small fraction of the city's area; in fact, it represents only a portion of Chicago's depressed areas. It is likely that many of the additional jobs and much of the real property that are attracted to the Empowerment Zone would have been located elsewhere in the city, perhaps even in another depressed area. Most likely the firms that will be attracted to the Empowerment Zone are those which are predisposed to locate somewhere in the inner city. (Below we provide an economic inventory of representative parts of the Empowerment Zone.)

It is quite possible, however, that the Empowerment Zone can attract some economic activity that otherwise would not have located in the inner city. For example, it is likely that some of the firms already located in the Empowerment Zone will be able to grow through the ability to compete more effectively with firms in the suburbs or in other parts of the country. It is also possible that the Empowerment Zone will attract new firms that otherwise would have been located outside Chicago's inner city. Such outcomes are possible, and that the Empowerment Zone programs should be designed so as to achieve them.

The expansion of jobs in the inner city is desirable since many inner-city residents are unemployed, underemployed, or not seeking work because they are discouraged about their chances. Unemployment means that the person is actively seeking work but cannot find work at the current wage rate. Unemployment is a serious problem in the inner city, but underemployment may be even more serious. An underemployed person is employed but is working at less than his or her capacity. Some part-time workers, for example, wish to work full-time. Many others work in jobs that do not make full use of their skills and abilities, and are paid less than they might be able to earn if better jobs were available. Finally, discouraged workers are those who would be drawn into the labor market if they thought jobs were available to them. Official data are collected on unemployment and on part-time workers, but we do not know how many people fall into the underemployed and discouraged categories. It is reasonable to assume, however, that a substantial number of people who earn very low wages are underemployed. These working people cannot lift themselves out of poverty but, if given the chance, would be capable of holding better jobs with higher pay.

The goal of increasing the employment of unemployed, under-employed, and discouraged workers has merit on the grounds of efficiency as well as equity. Unemployed and underemployed resources are wasted resources: Putting an unemployed or discouraged worker to work adds to society's available economic output at a cost that is the value of the worker's "leisure time." An obvious benefit is the reduction in the unemployment compensation or welfare payments that are paid to the unemployed person; let us calculate this precisely. Suppose a job is created for an unemployed worker at a wage rate of $6 per hour, and that the worker values his or her leisure time at $2.50 per hour. Assume that the unemployed worker has been receiving $350 per month in welfare payments. The worker now earns an income of $960 per month (160 hours of work per month). Previously the monthly income had been $350, and the leisure time that is given up to work has a worth of $400 per month. The worker is now better off by $210 per month, and the rest of society is better off by $350 per month from the reduction in welfare benefits. The benefits therefore total $560 per month. Another approach is to think that the worker, while unemployed, was producing leisure time worth $400 per month. Employment at a wage of $6 per hour produces output worth $960 per month, for a net gain of $560. In this case society chooses to distribute this net gain by reducing the welfare payment to zero. This distributional scheme results in a gain of $210 for the worker and $350 for the rest of society.

The case of the underemployed worker is essentially the same. Society gives up the value of whatever the underemployed worker had been producing, but gains the value of his or her new output. The new output is assumed to be of greater value than the old output. If the underemployed worker received no welfare payments before becoming fully employed, the net gain to society is in the form of increased wages (after taxes) and increased income taxes.

In addition to the direct employment effect (namely the increase in employment), output and income in the inner city may have a multiplier effect on the local economy that will result in putting more unemployed, underemployed, or discouraged workers to work. The calculation of such multiplier benefits is the same as for the direct benefits of employment discussed above.

Will the Empowerment Zone program lead to a net increase in the employment of unemployed, underemployed, or discouraged workers who otherwise have low incomes? It will do so if:

1. Jobs are attracted to the Empowerment Zone that otherwise would not have been located in the inner city, and if

2. Some of those jobs are filled by these groups, or if the multiplier effects on the inner-city economy lead to increased employment of these groups.

The Empowerment Zone program will fail on grounds of both efficiency and equity if either of these conditions is not met. For example, suppose that new jobs are created in the inner city, but that they are all taken by middle-class workers who live in the suburbs. There has been no net increase in unemployed, underemployed, or discouraged workers who live in the inner city, either directly or indirectly (through the local multiplier effect).

As a second example, suppose that no new jobs are created in the inner city, but that firms in the Empowerment Zone fire some workers who do not live in the Zone and replace them with Zone residents to take advantage of the tax credit granted for hiring Zone residents. Who are the workers that have been fired? It is likely that they are also inner-city residents because they are already working for the firms in question and because they hold jobs that can be taken by residents of the Empowerment Zone. Therefore it is probable that equity has not been improved.

The way to ensure that the Empowerment Zone program enhances both economic efficiency and equity is to meet both criteria: net job creation in the inner city and increased employment of the unemployed, underemployed, or discouraged workers of the inner city. The next step is to consider whether the Empowerment Zone in fact can generate these outcomes.

The Illinois Enterprise Zone Program

One way to determine the likely effects of the business incentives in the Empowerment Zone program is to look back at the economic effects of the Illinois Enterprise Zone program. The federal Empowerment Zone program is descended from the original idea of a federal enterprise zone program. Enterprise zones first were proposed in 1978 by Sir Geoffrey Howe, a Conservative member of the British House of Commons who later served in the Thatcher government. Stuart Butler, a researcher with the Heritage Foundation, introduced the idea in the United States in 1979; Jack Kemp, formerly a conservative Republican congressman and a former Secretary of HUD, immediately became a strong advocate of the proposal.

The basic idea of an enterprise zone program is to provide tax incentives and regulatory relief to businesses located in depressed parts of urban areas. Kemp and his congressional colleagues did not succeed in creating a federal program while the Republicans held the White House, but the idea was received enthusiastically by many state and local officials. Enterprise zone programs now exist in some form in at least 37 states; Green's (1991) book provides a detailed overview of these programs.

The first bill to create an enterprise zone program in Illinois was introduced in the legislature in 1979. The original proposal was politically too conservative for many lawmakers; three years of negotiation and compromise were needed to formulate a program that was acceptable to the legislature and the governor. The Illinois Enterprise Zone Act took effect on December 7, 1982, and the first eight enterprise zones were certified on July 1, 1983. As stated in the Act, the purpose of the program is to "explore ways and means of stimulating business and industrial growth and retention in depressed areas of the state by means of relaxed government controls and tax incentives for those areas." The Illinois Department of Commerce and Community Affairs (DCCA) is the state agency responsible for administering the program, but local governments, in conjunction with local community groups, select program objectives and administer the program day to day.

The original Enterprise Zone Act limited enterprise zones to 10 contiguous square miles, limited the life of a zone to 20 years, and authorized the creation of eight enterprise zones per year for six years. From 1983 to 1991 the Act was amended each year to allow the creation of more enterprise zones; there are now 90 such zones in Illinois. Except in two special cases, DCCA awarded enterprise zone designation on the basis of a high unemployment rate (20 percent greater than the state average), low income, poverty, or population loss.

The incentives offered in enterprise zones by the State of Illinois are listed in Table 6.1. Other incentives such as property tax abatements and reduced rates for building permits are offered in addition by local and county governments. The most frequently used components of the program are the sales tax exemption for building supplies, the state income tax credit for investment in machinery, equipment, or buildings, and local property tax abatements. Consequently the program tends to promote investment in structures.

Table 6.1

Illinois Enterprise Zone Incentives

---

1. Exemption of the 7 percent sales tax on building materials used by business in an enterprise zone.
2. State income tax credit of 0.5 percent for investment in machinery, equipment, or buildings used in the enterprise zone.
3. State income tax deduction for (a) interest received by financial institutions on loans for enterprise zone developements, (b) dividends received from a corporation conducting essentially all of its business in a zone, and (c) contributions (at double the value) for an approved project being undertaken by a Designated Zone Organization.
4. State income tax credit of $500 for each job created in a zone if at least five jobs are created and certified dislocated or disadvantaged workers are hired to fill them.
5. Exemption of state utility taxes and state sales taxes on materials and machinery used in manufacturing processes or pollution control (available to certain qualified large businesses only).

DCCA recognized at the outset that the incentives offered by the program were not designed to have large effects on investment and employment. Yet it was hoped that economic activity would be stimulated somewhat in depressed areas of the state, even if the result was some reduction in economic growth elsewhere of the state. One of the original goals of the program was the promotion of a more equitable spatial distribution of growth in the local tax base and employment. Is there evidence that the program stimulated economic activity in the enterprise zones in and near the city of Chicago?

By 1986, twelve enterprise zones had been certified in Cook County: six in the city of Chicago and six in the southern and western suburbs. The areas included in the federal Empowerment Zone are also included in enterprise zones. The suburban enterprise zones are located in Chicago Heights, Cicero, Harvey, McCook/Hodgkins, Summit/Bedford Park, and the Cal-Sag Channel area (Blue Island, Robbins, and other communities). The study by McDonald (1993), which covered the period from 1985 to 1989, compared employment trends in the areas covered by these enterprise zones with trends in otherwise similar areas of Cook County.

Statistical analysis revealed that the Enterprise Zone program had no impact on total private employment during the 1985-1989 period. However, employment growth in the distribution sector (transportation and wholesale trade) was much higher in enterprise zones than in other areas of the county during this period: Employment growth in this sector averaged 32.5 percent in the enterprise zone areas, compared with 5.4 percent in otherwise similar areas. This growth in the distribution sector probably occurred because the property tax incentive offered by Cook County concentrates on this sector in enterprise zones. A property tax incentive is offered to manufacturers located anywhere in the county. Industrial property in an enterprise zone that is not engaged in manufacturing production activities (such as transportation of manufactured products or wholesale trade in such products) is eligible for an incentive that lowers the property tax by 56 percent for eight years and by 17 percent for four additional years. This incentive applies to new, substantially rehabilitated, and formerly abandoned property. In 1985-1989, other types of businesses were not eligible for a property tax incentive in Cook County. McDonald (1993) found that enterprise zone designation had no impact on employment in manufacturing, retail trade, or services (including financial services).

A survey of firms located in four Cook County enterprise zones found that program participants mentioned the importance of the property tax incentive. Some 61 percent of the firms that used this incentive (and responded to the survey) stated that this feature was a critical factor in the decision to invest. In contrast, only 17% of firms that used any enterprise zone incentive responded that an incentive was critically important.

What do we learn from this examination of the Illinois Enterprise Zone program? First, the program had no effect on total employment in the zones. The program succeeded in attracting employment in one sector (distribution), which was experiencing growth, was willing to consider locating in an enterprise zone, and received a fairly sizable subsidy (including a property tax reduction). Yet the program really has little or nothing to offer to businesses in sectors that are experiencing declines in employment. It subsidizes the growth of a business but offers nothing to prevent or reduce decline. The state income tax credit for investment in machinery and equipment (and buildings) can help the firm to modernize its operations, but this tax credit is only .5 percent of the investment spending.

Second, it is clear that the original focus of the program has been lost. With 90 enterprise zones in existence throughout the state, the program can hardly claim to concentrate on depressed areas. It will be less successful at stimulating investment and employment in depressed areas if other parts of the state also contain enterprise zones.

What do these two basic lessons imply for the Empowerment Zone program? First, the Empowerment Zone program places less emphasis on subsidizing growth than does the Illinois Enterprise Zone program. The provision for accelerated depreciation can be used by a qualified firm to update its plant and equipment, and the tax credit for wages paid to Zone residents can be used at once by any employer in the Zone. The wage tax credit is a particularly innovative feature.

Second, there are (so far) only six Empowerment Zones in the nation. In my view, any expansion of the program by HUD must be conducted slowly and carefully, in contrast to the Illinois program. These considerations suggest that the Empowerment Zone program has the potential to produce the desired results to some degree.

An Economic Inventory of Chicago's Empowerment Zone

In this section we briefly survey the existing economic resources in Chicago's Empowerment Zone. We use this inventory as a basis for some preliminary thoughts about the likely results of the Empowerment Zone program.

Table 6.2 displays basic data (as of 1990) about the 200,000 people who live in the Zone. Only 46.2 percent of men age 18 and over were employed, 14.8 percent were unemployed, and 39.0 percent were not in the labor force. These numbers indicate a severely depressed area. Also, only 30.7 percent of the women were employed (and 59.0 percent were not in the labor force); this finding runs counter to the recent increase in the proportion of women who work outside the home. Furthermore, for persons employed in 1989 the average earnings from wages and/or self-employment were only $15,760. (The official poverty line for a family of four was $12,675 in 1989.) Granted, we find considerable variation around this average; it includes part-time workers who earn very little as well as college graduates who make good salaries.

Table 6.2

Characteristics of Empowerment Zone Residents: 1990

```
        Employment Status (Age 18 and over)
           Males
                Employed            46.2%
                Unemployed          14.8
                Not in labor force  39.0

           Females
                Employed            30.7
                Unemployed          10.3
                Not in labor force  59.0

        Educational Attainment (Age 25 and over)
           0-11 years               55.9%
           High school graduate     23.5
           Some college             15.8
           College graduate          3.0
           Graduate degree           1.6

        Race/Ethnicity
           Hispanic                 24.2%
                White                        6.7
                Black                         .3
                Other                       17.2

           Non-Hispanic             75.8
                White                        4.0
                Black                       71.5
                Other                        .4
```

Source: Census of Population, 1990.

The next entry in Table 6.2 shows one important reason for the low employment and earnings of Zone residents: 55.9 percent of the adults (age 25 and over) had not graduated from high school. Although 20.4

percent had attended some college classes, only 4.6 percent graduated; only 22.5 percent of those who had attended college received degrees. In short, the adults who live in the Zone are grouped heavily at the lower end of the educational attainment scale. Numerous recent studies of the income distribution in the United States, such as Danziger and Gottschalk (1995), have demonstrated that high school dropouts have experienced the greatest declines in wages in the past 20 years, that the economic returns to a college education have increased, and that some training beyond high school is becoming increasingly important for workers who do not graduate from college.

The final portion of Table 6.2 shows that the residents of the Zone are almost entirely members of minority groups. Non-Hispanic blacks make up 71.5 percent of the population; the Hispanic population is 24.2 percent of the total. Employment prospects for Zone residents are reduced further, insofar as these groups face discrimination in the labor market.

In addition to low levels of employment and earnings, Zone residents exhibit other forms of nonattachment to today's economy. Table 6.3 displays some results of a survey of basic household financial information conducted by the Metropolitan Chicago Information Center. The survey shows that few Zone residents use a checking account, a savings account, or a general credit card such as VISA or MasterCard. The survey estimates that only 10 percent of the households own their homes; fully 42 percent receive housing assistance, either in the form of public housing or as a rent subsidy. In short, the Zone residents are in great need of an economic boost. Yet because of their low level of formal education, their ability to

Table 6.3

Household Characteristics: 1994

	Metropolitan Area	City of Chicago	Empowerment Zone
Checking account use	82%	65%	21%
Savings account use	75	62	26
General credit card use	70	54	13
Own home	61	39	10
Thinking of moving	36	44	47
Receives housing aid	9	12	42

Source: Metropolitan Chicago Information Center.

take advantage of an increase in economic opportunity is unclear. I believe that the Empowerment Zone program should include an assessment of the residents' educational needs as they relate to the general skills needed for the jobs in and near the Zone.

Table 6.4 shows a portion of the inventory of employment in the Empowerment Zone. The table contains employment data by broad industry category for the postal zone with the largest amount of employment in each of the three portions of the Empowerment Zone. These three postal zone areas are the largest centers of employment in the Zone; therefore they indicate the kind of employment that will be available in the Zone in the future. We examine each area in turn.

By far the largest concentration of employment in the southern portion of the Empowerment Zone is located in the Stockyards area. Employment here is weighted very heavily toward manufacturing and, to a lesser extent, wholesale trade and transportation. Manufacturing jobs in the area were devastated by the deep recession of the early 1980s; employment fell by 42.8 percent from 1979 to 1986. Since that time, however, some of that loss has been recovered: The area added 1,182 manufacturing jobs between 1986 and 1993, an increase of 13.2 percent. More highly detailed data (not shown) reveal that jobs were added in furniture and fixtures, transportation equipment, paper and allied products, and plastics. The largest manufacturing industry in the area is food products, which employed 2,638 workers in 1993. Employment in this industry has remained fairly stable since it experienced a sharp decline in the early 1980s. Employment in wholesale trade increased by 5.4 percent from 1986 to 1993, and jobs in TCU (transportation, communications, and utilities) rose 54.9 percent over this period to 1,980. These last findings mirror the results from the study of the Illinois Enterprise Zone program that we discussed above.

In short, the Stockyards area recently has enjoyed considerable success in attracting employment in manufacturing and distribution. The increase in manufacturing employment in the area is especially notable because manufacturing jobs in the six-county metropolitan area declined by 1.7 percent over the 1986-1993 period. Can the Stockyards area continue to

Table 6.4

Major Employment Centers in the Empowerment Zone

Stockyards

	1979	1986	1993	
Manufacturing	15,694	8,978	10,160	43.1%
Durables	5,619	4,044	4,738	
Nondurables	10,075	4,934	5,422	
Nonmanufacturing				
Construction	1,127	790	1,031	4.4
TCU*	1,733	1,278	1,980	8.4
Wholesale trade	4,821	3,132	3,300	14.0
Retail trade	**	**	3,065	13.0
FIRE***	807	920	381	1.6
Health services		123	115	0.5
Other services	{2,646}	3,534	3,515	14.9
Total	**	**	23,551	

Pilsen

	1979	1986	1993	
Manufacturing	9,581	7,346	7,160	27.2%
Durables	5,155	3,022	3,209	
Nondurables	4,426	4,324	3,951	
Nonmanufacturing				
Construction	565	561	780	3.0
TCU*	4,472	1,965	2,173	8.2
Wholesale trade	7,343	6,129	6,040	22.9
Retail trade	2,306	1,867	2,800	10.5
FIRE***	592	364	384	1.5
Health services		2,281	3,408	12.9
Other services	{2,398}	2,298	3,597	13.6
Total	27,257	22,810	26,352	

Postal Zone 60612 (West Side)

	1979	1986	1993	
Manufacturing	7,818	5,846	5,019	23.7%
Durables	5,396	3,868	3,543	
Nondurables	2,422	1,978	1,476	
Nonmanufacturing				
Construction	905	1,034	285	1.3
TCU*	728	344	327	1.5
Wholesale trade	1,906	1,751	1,724	8.1
Retail trade	961	712	778	3.7
FIRE***	539	270	139	0.7
Health Services		8,659	10,654	50.3
Other services	{17,374}	2,324	2,244	10.6
Total	30,231	21,160	21,177	

-----

*TCU stands for transportation, communication, and utilities.
** Data for 1979 and 1986 were not accurate.
*** FIRE stands for finance, insurance, and real estate.
Source: *Where Workers Work*, Illinois Department of Employment Security, 1979, 1986, and 1993.

perform so well? If any inner-city area can attract additional jobs in manufacturing and distribution, the Stockyards area appears to be a leading candidate.

Table 6.4 shows that employment in the Pilsen area is also weighted toward manufacturing, wholesale trade, and TCU (transportation, communication, and utilities). Employment in these sectors did not change much between 1986 and 1993. This fact is actually fairly good news: A stable employment base in these basic sectors means that a continuing stream of job openings will be available as workers retire or move on to other jobs. The major manufacturing industries in Pilsen are food products, furniture and fixtures, and fabricated metals. All three of these industries displayed modest employment growth between 1986 and 1993. However, the retail trade and service sectors have grown rapidly in recent years. Table 6.4 shows that the entire service sector almost doubled in size between 1979 and 1986, and that growth continued from 1986 to 1993. Growth also has occurred in health services and in other parts of the service sector.

Postal zone 60612 is located on the West Side, but only about one-half of this zone is included in the Empowerment Zone. Zone 60612 covers the West Side medical center (which includes Cook County Hospital, Rush-Presbyterian-St. Luke's Medical Center, and the University of Illinois Medical Center), but the medical center is not part of the Empowerment Zone. However, it has the largest concentration of employment on the West Side. The data in Table 6.4 do not include employment in the public sector (e.g., Cook County Hospital and the University of Illinois), but the table still shows the concentration in health services in this area.

Table 6.4 also shows that this area has a sizable manufacturing employment base. Most of this activity is located in the Empowerment Zone, but jobs in this sector declined by 14.1percent from 1986 to 1993. The area also had 1,724 jobs in wholesale trade in 1993, essentially the same as in 1986. Postal zone 60612 contains the new United Center, the home of the Chicago Blackhawks and Chicago Bulls professional sports teams. The United Center represents an opportunity for businesses that serve the patrons of the facility; such businesses may be attracted by the Empowerment Zone incentives.

The rest of the West Side portion of the Empowerment Zone is located to the west of postal zone 60612 in Garfield Park and Austin. These areas have declining employment bases and large amounts of vacant land.

What preliminary conclusions can be drawn by examining the existing employment in the Empowerment Zone? One immediate conclusion is that the employment situation is far less bleak than might have been imagined. The data also show that the three parts of the Zone are different: All three areas still have sizable employment bases in manufacturing and distribution, but in recent years this employment base has grown in the Stockyards area, has remained stable in Pilsen, and has declined on the West Side. Pilsen has a large and growing service sector, and both the West Side and Pilsen are close to the huge West Side medical center (which is not included in the Empowerment Zone). Furthermore, the West Side contains the United Center.

In one way, however, all three portions of the Zone are the same; they have almost no employment in the FIRE (finance, insurance, and real estate) sector. As we saw in Table 6.3, residents of the Zone hardly use even the basic financial services. Given the new Empowerment Zone incentives, creative providers of basic financial services surely must see an opportunity to enter these greatly under served areas. Meanwhile we should watch for job opportunities in manufacturing and distribution (especially in the Stockyards and Pilsen areas) and in services (especially health services in Pilsen and in the nearby West Side medical center).

What Will the Future Bring?

How many and what kinds of job opportunities will appear in the Empowerment Zone? Forecasting for an entire metropolitan area is not difficult, but such forecasts often are unreliable. In the early 1960s, for example, the Chicago Area Transportation Study projected a population of 11 million for the Chicago metropolitan area by 1980. That figure, however, overshot the mark by about 4 million (roughly the population of metropolitan Detroit). Several forecasts of employment by broad industry category are available for the Chicago metropolitan area; they range from optimistic to pessimistic. Even more difficult is the task of forecasting reliably for a small portion of a metropolitan area; we will not attempt to make such forecasts here.

Forecasters of the national economy generally have better track records than forecasters of local economies. The economists at the U.S. Department of Labor have a respectable record for predicting employment changes by major industry category, and in November 1995 they issued their two-yearly official forecast. This forecast is "official" in the sense that it will serve as the basis for employment forecasts by each of the states in their efforts to make the best use of federal job training funds. The forecast is summarized briefly in Table 6.5.

The U.S. Department of Labor projects a decline in the rate of employment growth for the 1994-2005 period as compared with the previous 15 years. This drop in the annual rate of employment growth from 1.6 percent to 1.3 percent is due largely to the expected decline in the growth rate of the labor force; all of the baby boomers now have reached adulthood. (The year 1979 is used as the base year for this comparison because it was a peak year for the business cycle.) However, the rate of decline projected for manufacturing employment is smaller than the actual rate of decline over the previous 15 years, a period that includes the deep recession of the early 1980s. In recent years American manufacturers have become more productive and more competitive in world markets. The former trend tends to reduce employment; the latter trend increases employment. The net outcome is projected to be an annual decline of .7 percent per year. The fact that the annual rate of decline in manufacturing employment is projected to be almost as great as it was during 1979-1994 is not a good sign because that 15-year period includes the 12.4 percent drop in manufacturing jobs that occurred during 1979-1983 and the smaller decline that took place during the recession of the early 1990s.

Employment growth in services is projected to be a robust 3.0 percent per year, down from 3.9 percent for the previous 15 years. The other sectors are projected to show more modest rates of employment growth, ranging from .6 percent per year in TCU, wholesale trade, and FIRE to 1.1 percent in retail trade. With the exception of construction, all of these other sectors are projected to have lower rates of employment growth than during the 1979-1994 period. The declines in the growth rates projected for FIRE (from 2.2 percent to .6 percent) and for retail trade (from 2.1 percent to 1.1 percent) are particularly sharp.

Table 6.5 sends a clear message: The new jobs in the United States are projected to be largely in the service sector and in retail trade. Retail wages generally are low; pay in the service sector varies greatly, depending on the specific job and the education and training needed for the job. The overall outlook for jobs in manufacturing is not promising, although specific industries no doubt will do well. For example, if the

Table 6.5

Actual and Projected Employment in the U.S.
by Major Industry Division

	Annual Growth Rates Actual: 1979-1994	Projected: 1994-2005	Share in 1994	Growth 1994-2005 (1000s)
Manufacturing	-0.9	-0.7	16.1%	-1,313
Durables	-1.3	-1.0	9.2	-1,141
Nondurables	-0.4	-0.2	6.9	-172
Nonmanufacturing				
Construction	0.8	0.9	4.4	490
TCU*	1.0	0.6	5.3	425
Wholesale trade	1.1	0.6	5.4	419
Retail trade	2.1	1.1	18.0	2,657
FIRE**	2.2	0.6	6.1	439
Services	3.9	3.0	27.2	12,018
Government	1.3	0.9	15.4	1,873
Total nonfarm	1.6	1.3	100.0	16,846

*TCU stands for transportation, communications, and utilities.
**FIRE stands for finance, insurance, and real estate.

Source: *Monthly Labor Review*, November 1995, p. 47.

market for high-tech electronics products (such as cellular phones and personal computers) continues to grow, Chicago-area firms such as Motorola will flourish. (An analysis of specific industries is beyond the scope of this essay.) Nationwide employment opportunities in TCU, wholesale trade, and FIRE are projected to grow more slowly than in the previous 15 years. However, Chicago is a national center of transportation, wholesale trade, and financial services. Perhaps this metropolitan area can continue to capitalize on its advantages in these sectors and surpass the national averages in job creation.

In view of the national employment forecast, what conclusions can we reach regarding employment growth in Chicago's Empowerment Zone? We offer these six tentative conclusions:

1. Given that total manufacturing employment is projected to decline, a reasonably attainable goal is to retain the manufacturing employment base in the Empowerment Zone. The incentives provided by the program should give the Zone an edge in retaining jobs and avoiding major layoffs. In particular, the accelerated depreciation and the tax-exempt bond features of the program may help some firms to update their operations, and the wage tax credit for hiring Zone residents can help to control labor costs. Retention of the manufacturing employment base will create a steady stream of job openings as workers depart.

2. Given the strong record of employment growth in some of parts of the service sector in Pilsen, this area seems poised to participate in the strong growth that is projected. Further research is needed to find the specific areas of strength. Health care clearly is one such category, but the others must be identified so that job training and job counseling programs can be used effectively. Some parts of the service sector also may offer opportunities for starting new businesses, which also involve hiring Zone residents.

3. The distribution sector (TCU and wholesale trade) has a strong presence in all parts of the Empowerment Zone, and this sector responded to the incentives offered by the Illinois Enterprise Zone program. Nationwide employment growth in distribution is projected to slow down, but it is still reasonable to suggest that it will provide some employment gains for the Empowerment Zone. A detailed study of occupations in this sector was conducted for Cook County by NCI Research (1995); this report can serve as a guide for education and job training programs. The

findings in the report are summarized briefly in the appendix to this chapter.

4. Retail trade has shown strength in Pilsen. Although retail jobs generally pay rather poorly, a steady job in this industry still may be able to lift a family out of poverty. In addition, opportunities exist for entrepreneurs in this field (and in others, of course).

5. This study has revealed a basic lack of financial services in the Empowerment Zone. Given the business incentives in the program, this situation presents opportunities to offer essential banking, insurance, real estate, and other services.

6. A major potential problem is the low educational background of many Zone residents. Residents must improve their basic skills in order to take advantage of job opportunities. An assessment of the residents' educational and training needs should be the first order of business for the Empowerment Zone program coordinators.

One final matter is knowledge of the Empowerment Zone program, its provisions, and its boundaries. Many employers in the Illinois Enterprise Zone areas are not aware that they are located in such a zone. One important duty is to make every possible effort to inform firms in the Empowerment Zone about the provisions of the program, and to tell everyone in the metropolitan area that if one lives in the Zone, one's Empowerment Zone employer is eligible for the wage tax credit.

Appendix 6A
Skills for Jobs in the Distribution Sector

Researchers at NCI Research and Northern Illinois University, in collaboration with industry representatives and providers of job training programs, have completed an intensive investigation of the skills that are needed to perform some of the basic jobs in the distribution sector [NCI Research (1995)]. The distribution sector is defined to include the transportation and wholesale trade industries. An investigation of all of the occupations in the sector produced a short list of occupation clusters that represent real employment opportunities for workers with more limited educational backgrounds. An occupation cluster is a group of more specific occupations that shares common educational and basic skill requirements. The four occupation clusters identified are:

- Vehicle operator/driver,
- Customer service representative,
- Dispatchers/internal material schedulers, non-air traffic, and
- Transportation mechanics and repair technicians.

Jobs in the first three clusters only require a high school diploma or less, and jobs in the fourth cluster require a high school diploma and some post-secondary training.

The specific occupational skills and the general skills required for jobs in each of these clusters were investigated through survey research methods. Major gaps in the skills of applicants were also identified. The product of the research is a system that can be used to communicate to providers of job training programs (e.g., the City Colleges of Chicago) the specific and general skills that are really needed for these occupations. This system is called a skill-based local labor market information system. One objective of the system is to give job training providers the ability to certify that a graduate of a training program meets certain relevant skill standards (in much the same way that the ISO 9000 system is used to certify the quality of industrial products). Systems such as the one developed in the NCI Research report (1995) holds some promise for providing the critical labor market information links that are needed to enable workers such as the residents of the Empowerment Zone to gain the general and more specific training that will lead to a good job.

Chapter 7

Jobs and Poverty Alleviation in Chicago's Empowerment Zone

Nikolas Theodore

For decades, the intractable nature of inner-city economic distress has been a major challenge to shapers of public policy. The policy terrain is littered with failed attempts to alleviate poverty and increase economic activity in low-income urban neighborhoods. The mere mention of the best-known initiatives, such as the Model Cities program and urban renewal, draws the ire of communities and policy makers alike. As a result of these failures of public policy, conventional wisdom implies that large-scale revitalization initiatives cannot succeed.

Much of the failure of large-scale efforts has been attributed to the top-down planning and implementation of previous revitalization programs. Communities rarely have been at the center of goal setting, project design, and implementation. As a result, revitalization plans have been discon-nected from the very people they were intended to benefit. Unlike previous federal initiatives, the Empowerment Zone/Enterprise Com-munity (EZ/EC) program is designed to be community-centered. The EZ/EC program is based on an understanding that "residents themselves

... are the most important element of revitalization" (U.S. Department of Housing and Urban Development 1994:9). To emphasize this point, the EZ/EC planning guidebook calls for community-based partnerships and broad participation by all segments of the community. Because revitalization plans are to emanate from community-based organizations and other neighborhood institutions, the EZ/EC program provides a unique opportunity to implement and evaluate various initiatives targeted to the most economically disadvantaged neighborhoods. In this way, what is learned from activities conducted under the EZ/EC process can inform future urban policy making and social service delivery throughout the nation.

The EZ/EC guidebook states that the "first priority in revitalizing distressed communities is to create economic opportunities—jobs and work—for all residents" (U.S. Department of Housing and Urban Development 1994:8). In addressing this priority, the Chicago EZ/EC application established multiple goals targeted toward alleviating poverty (City of Chicago 1994):

- Build on the existing community skill base to develop appropriate living-wage jobs with potential for advancement (p. 34);
- Expand job training services (p.34);
- Link businesses and community-based organizations with job development and training projects to meet the needs of zone residents (p.48);
- Support neighborhood enterprise development (p.49).

In this chapter, we examine the economic context for neighborhood revitalization activities in the Chicago Empowerment Zone. We focus primarily on the possibilities for strengthening connections between neighborhood employment, local business development, and community employment assistance services. To begin, we summarize the relationship between the regional economy and employment opportunities for inner-city residents. Next we consider issues of labor supply and demand in the Grand Boulevard community area located in the Chicago Empowerment Zone: first, we analyze the neighborhood residents' work histories and job search strategies; second, we examine the employment needs and hiring practices of neighborhood businesses. The strategies and practices of workers and firms then are compared to the goals of the Chicago EZ/EC plan submitted to and approved by the U.S. Department of Housing and Urban Development. Finally, we consider implications for policy making, program design, and service delivery.

Uneven Development and the Decline in Inner-City Employment

The last 20 years have been a time of rapid economic change. The trends are well known: job growth in producer and consumer services, employment losses in high-wage manufacturing industries, growth in western and southern regions, and decline in the older urban centers of the northeast and midwest. In region after region, change has caused tremendous economic hardships as industrial restructuring has led to large reductions in the workforce. After the 1990-1991 recession, however, the employment picture began to improve as overall employment reached the highest level in history. In fact, even the regions that had been hit hardest by economic restructuring saw total employment rise and unemployment rates fall sharply. Yet in the midst of job growth and seemingly tight labor markets, inner-city poverty rates continued to increase and labor force participation rates remained low.

One explanation for inner-city residents' lower economic well-being is that restructuring has led to uneven development within regions. In many metropolitan areas, central-city disinvestment and the suburbanization of business activity have dramatically reordered the spatial distribution of employment. In inner-city neighborhoods, shifts in economic activity have left a legacy of extensive job loss, long-term unemployment, and persistent poverty. As a result of these changes, large numbers of low-income families live in neighborhoods plagued by business losses and the deterioration of employment opportunities. It is likely that as metropolitan economies continue to be reshaped, inner-city neighborhoods will struggle to retain their employment bases and large numbers of residents will find it difficult to secure work.

The long-term unemployed have become concentrated increasingly in neighborhoods that are physically and socially isolated from emerging employment centers (Kasinitz and Rosenberg 1994; Wilson 1987). When combined with the decline of inner-city economies, this isolation creates great hardships for residents. Workers with few employment opportunities near their homes are forced to find employment in distant job centers. Commuting may be costly in time and money and is not always feasible from a transportation standpoint, while residential relocation closer to job sites is limited because of discrimination and may not be financially possible for low-wage workers.

In addition to the costs and family disruptions associated with finding and retaining work at distant job sites, workers' access to job-search information has been found to diminish across space (Hanson and Pratt 1992). Reliance on informal methods of locating jobs, such as everyday interactions with friends and neighbors, limits the flow of labor-market information to areas centered around the home (Hanson and Pratt 1995).

Consequently, inner-city job seekers have limited knowledge of suburban job opportunities. Furthermore, employers are well aware of the geography of local labor markets and express their preferences for different types of workers through recruitment and hiring practices (Hanson and Pratt 1992; Kirschenman and Neckerman 1991). Employers' recruitment strategies, such as word-of-mouth notification about opportunities and the avoidance of workers who live far from job sites, create highly localized workforces.

Diminishing employment levels in inner-city neighborhoods, combined with workers' and employers' preferences for shorter-distance commuting, have severely undermined inner-city workers' employment prospects. New labor market entrants who cannot find steady jobs see their employment futures grow dim because they cannot establish a work history and develop their skills. More experienced workers whose jobs have been eliminated by restructuring have seen their position in the labor market erode because they are unable to maintain continuous employment and capitalize on their skills.

Job seekers who are unemployed for long periods often lose their attachment to the labor market as human capital and job-search efforts go unrewarded. Some workers accept jobs that require less skill than they possess. Others participate in the informal economy as self-employed workers, day laborers, or odd-job holders. Still others become discouraged and discontinue their job search. These forms of joblessness and under-employment expose workers to economic insecurity and ultimately weaken local economies.

Employment Experiences of Grand Boulevard Residents

Many areas of Chicago have been hit particularly hard by economic restructuring and uneven development. One such area, the Grand Boulevard neighborhood located on the South Side of Chicago, is similar to many other inner-city communities. Throughout the 1970s and 1980s, rates of employment decline and business loss were among the highest in the city (Theodore and Taylor 1991), as were poverty and unemployment rates (Wilson 1987).

As we show in the following sections, the Grand Boulevard labor force is characterized by limited work experience. In addition, employment opportunities in neighborhood businesses are few in number, pay poorly, and rarely offer opportunities for advancement. Furthermore, the role of community organizations in preparing the labor force and helping job seekers to find work is unclear. Success in accessing suburban employment centers has been limited, and few neighborhood firms actually look to community organizations to find potential workers. In an effort to improve their effectiveness as labor-market intermediaries, many community organizations are turning to the surrounding areas as a source of employment opportunities. Increasingly these organizations are recognizing that many less highly skilled workers will take their first steps in the labor market locally.

The economic circumstances that confront Grand Boulevard residents indicate the challenges facing community organizations and policy makers who are involved, through the EZ/EC process, in designing strategies to reverse economic decline and promote a higher standard of living among inner-city residents. In the next section, to clarify the nature of these circumstances, we examine 1990 census data and discuss the results of a survey of Grand Boulevard residents regarding their work histories, job search strategies, and education and training experiences.[1]

Findings from the 1990 Census and Resident Survey[2]
Employment Status

Data from the 1990 Census show that the labor force in the Grand Boulevard community area has been beset by high unemployment rates, low levels of labor force participation, and widespread underemployment (U.S. Department of Commerce 1992). The unemployment rate among Grand Boulevard residents was 34.1 percent, more than three times as high as the rate for the city of Chicago as a whole. In addition, the level of worker discouragement appears to be high: Nearly two-thirds of neighborhood residents age 16 and older were not in the labor force, an indication that they were not actively seeking employment. Among the employed residents, a substantial portion worked either part-time or part of the year; only 37.5 percent held full-year, full-time jobs.

The residents' employment difficulties are reflected in low income levels and a high incidence of poverty. The 1989 median household income in Grand Boulevard was $7,908, and fewer than one-fifth of the households reported an annual income of more than $20,000. Further-more, nearly 60 percent of Grand Boulevard households reported that they received no wage or salary income, and 64.7 percent of the residents were below the poverty line. In short, Grand Boulevard is a community where the majority of adult workers compete for low-paid, often part-time employment and therefore are engaged in a constant struggle to provide for their families.

Education and Training

The labor force in the Grand Boulevard neighborhood is characterized by low educational attainment. More than one-half (54.6 percent) of persons age 25 years and older had not completed high school. Of those who received a high school diploma, only 17.5 percent went on to receive an associate's, bachelor's, or other postsecondary degree. Among survey respondents, few adults (5.8 percent) currently were enrolled in school, and none were enrolled in a job training program.

Workers living in Grand Boulevard rarely participate in job training programs. Furthermore, most have not had access to intensive on-the-job training: Only 22.1 percent of the respondents reported that they had received on-the-job training lasting longer than two weeks. This suggests that few residents have benefited from employers' investments in their workforce and that the types of employment held by many workers do not require significant job-specific training.

Occupations

Overall, limited schooling and the lack of access to job training have restricted workers to competing for entry-level jobs. Recent and current employment by Grand Boulevard neighborhood residents is concentrated in low-paying, entry-level occupations.

The jobs typically held by Grand Boulevard residents require only limited skills and little work experience. The most common occupations are janitors, cleaners, and maids, followed by secretaries, receptionists, clerks, nursing assistants, and security guards. Few residents hold managerial or professional jobs. It is not clear whether residents possess higher-level skills but cannot capitalize on these skills because of inadequate employment opportunities.[3] Possibly workers must settle for

Table 7.1

Top Occupations of Grand Boulevard Residents

Occupation	Percent
Janitors, cleaners, and maids	11.7
Sectetaries, receptionists, and clerks	10.3
Nursing assistants	5.8
Security guards	5.8
Short order cooks, food preparation, and wait staff	5.8
Cashiers	4.9
Hand packers and assemblers	4.5
Teachers' aides	4.5
Laborers and handlers	4.5

Source: Chicago Urban League survey of Grand Boulevard residents, 1995.

entry-level positions for which they are overqualified because higher-skilled jobs are not available to neighborhood residents.

As indicated by the type and wages of residents' three most recent jobs, few Grand Boulevard workers have progressed along a path into jobs that require higher-level skills or reward them with higher pay. Furthermore, only 7.6 percent of respondents stated that their current employer had given them a promotion that increased their pay. These findings suggest that few opportunities for advancement are available to Grand Boulevard residents who hold low-skilled jobs, and that wage stagnation among these workers is common.

Job Search Strategies

Job seekers typically engage in a variety of strategies in their search for employment. Grand Boulevard residents who reported that they were currently looking for work used several different approaches. The most common methods were asking friends and relatives about job opportunities (85.2 percent) and looking at "help wanted" advertisements in newspapers (80.9 percent). Approximately 40 percent of job seekers reported that they contacted employers directly or looked for "help wanted" signs. Community residents seldom sought assistance in job placement from established service providers. They used private employment agencies (21 percent), state employment services (19.1 percent), community organizations (17.9 percent), and school placement services (2.5 percent), but not to the same extent as informal strategies. Almost one-quarter (23.5 percent) contacted temporary help agencies.

The majority of job seekers search for work within the city of Chicago. Nearly three-quarters (73.5 percent) reported that they looked for work in Grand Boulevard, 85.2 percent said they looked in the central business district (the Loop), and 82.7 percent reported looking in other parts of Chicago. A substantial proportion (58.6 percent) said they had sought employment in a suburban area.

Grand Boulevard residents stated that their job search activities have taken them to various parts of the metropolitan area, but lack of access to private transportation often constrains the search. Only 28.8 percent used a private vehicle to conduct their job search; most respondents used some form of public transportation. Chicago Transit Authority buses were most common (82.8 percent), followed by the subway (46.6 percent). In contrast to the wide use of mass transit in the city of Chicago, job seekers rarely used suburban public transportation: Few residents used suburban bus (6.7

percent) or commuter rail services (3.7 percent). More than one-fifth of residents reported that they walked to look for work.

Among Grand Boulevard residents, the labor force possesses limited formal education, has received little job training, and is concentrated in low-paying, entry-level occupations that offer few opportunities for advancement. These workers and the organizations that assist them are confronted by a labor market that provides too few low-level jobs to accommodate the large numbers of less skilled job seekers who need work (Carlson and Theodore 1995). As community initiatives attempt to increase employment opportunities for these workers, they must proceed with the understanding that successful programs may have to overcome an array of skill, wage, transportation, and other impediments to gainful employment.

Insofar as employment in the Grand Boulevard area can be promoted, transportation barriers can be largely eliminated. In the next section we consider the possibilities of expanding employment opportunities for Grand Boulevard residents in area firms.

Employment Practices of Grand Boulevard Businesses

A viable neighborhood business sector is an important component of inner-city economic revitalization. Neighborhood businesses give residents the opportunity to purchase necessities and other items. As residents spend money in the neighborhood, employment opportunities are created, and jobs often are filled by workers from the area. This process allows residents' spending to ripple through the local economy and generate additional economic activity. As a result, neighborhood businesses can be an important source of employment opportunities in a community, especially for entry-level workers and youths. Below we present the results of a survey of Grand Boulevard-area businesses regarding their employment needs and their hiring and training practices.[4]

Characteristics of Surveyed Businesses

Firms located in the Grand Boulevard area are primarily small-scale establishments that serve the neighborhood market. Many of these firms rely exclusively on neighborhood consumer demand as their source of business. Nearly one-half of the area businesses were in retail trade, one-fifth were in personal services and repair, and approximately 15 percent were eating and drinking establishments. In short, almost 85 percent of the firms were in industries that depend on neighborhood consumer demand.

The surveyed firms employed a total of 612 workers. As Table 7.2 illustrates, the largest proportion of employees in these firms worked in service (34.8 percent), sales (24.5 percent), and executive/managerial (16.8 percent) occupations. Overall, employment in Grand Boulevard-area firms is concentrated in the lowest occupational categories: Two-thirds of the employees in surveyed businesses held service, sales, and laborer positions.

Table 7.2

Occupational Distribution of Grand Boulevard Area Firms Surveyed

Occupational Category	Number of Employees	Percent
Executive/Managerial	103	16.8
Professional	42	6.9
Craft Workers	27	4.4
Machine Operator	29	4.7

Laborer/Handler	42	6.9
Sales	149	24.5
Transportation	7	1.1
Service	213	34.8
Total	612	100.1

Source: Results of a survey conducted by the Chicago Urban League and the Kenwood Oakland Community Organization, 1993.

Most of the firms in the Grand Boulevard area have been located in the neighborhood for a long time. Nearly one-third of the surveyed firms have been at their present location for more than 25 years. An additional 30 percent have been in their present location between 11 and 24 years, and almost 18 percent between six and 10 years. Only about 18 percent reported that they had been in their present location for five years or less. The average tenure of businesses in the area, 21.5 years, reflects the stability of those firms which have managed to survive despite neighborhood economic decline. In addition, it appears that few new business are starting operations there.

Hiring Due to Changes in Demand

Small firms, like many of those located in the Grand Boulevard area, have less highly developed internal labor markets than other firms.[5] Frequently the workforces of small firms are unskilled and semiskilled, and thus are concentrated in positions toward the lower end of the occupational hierarchy. Sometimes small businesses of this type require flexible labor markets to meet changes in demand. Because their internal workforce often cannot handle periodic increases in demand, the need for flexibility forces these firms into the external labor market. One response of small firms has been to develop a workforce in which core employees are hired as permanent, full-time workers, while additional contingent workers are brought in as needed and then released (Bosworth 1989). In such a core-contingent scenario, labor adjustments are made primarily through the contingent workforce as firms hire and lay off part-time and temporary workers depending on their need for additional labor.

Although the availability of low-skilled contingent workers offers several benefits to small firms, it also has limitations. On the one hand, the contingent workforce may give businesses access to more workers than would be possible otherwise. Employees can be brought in as needed to supplement the core workforce. In addition, the direct costs of maintaining a contingent workforce are relatively low because employee benefits typically are not offered to contingent workers and recruitment procedures are less involved than with core employees.

On the other hand, reliance on contingent workers pushes the average overall quality of the small firms' workforces even farther below that of larger firms. In retail establishments during the holiday season, for example, relative reductions in quality may not be much of a drawback. However, in industry sectors requiring higher levels of skill or experience, the disadvantages of relying on a contingent workforce are evident.

As might be expected, most of the surveyed firms responded to increases in demand by hiring part-time employees (60.6 percent) or temporary workers (15.2 percent). Overtime by existing employees was encouraged by only 27.3 percent of surveyed businesses. These figures support the conclusion that Grand Boulevard-area firms have adopted core-contingent strategies for managing labor needs. In addition, there are only modest employment opportunities as a result of employee turnover in area businesses. The surveyed firms predicted that annual employment growth would be less than 1 percent and that only about 5 percent of existing positions would become available as a result of turnover. Not surprisingly, higher levels of turnover were anticipated by retail trade and service establishments.

The operation of core-contingent strategies indicates only a limited potential for greater levels of permanent, full-time employment through existing firms in Grand Boulevard. An exception to this conclusion could be made in the case of new infusions of resident income that would greatly increase long-run consumer demand, if business-to-business purchases were to increase dramatically and consistently through the creation of new businesses that could supply existing firms, or if existing firms could obtain greater financial capital to expand operations.

Hiring of Neighborhood Residents

Grand Boulevard-area firms vary greatly in their reliance on neighborhood residents to supply their labor needs. Fifty percent of surveyed firms stated that at least three-quarters of their employees lived in the neighborhood. These businesses tended to be in the retail trade and service sectors, and typically were small businesses or franchises that served the neighborhood market. An additional 20 percent of surveyed firms reported that between one-half and three-quarters of their employees lived in the neighborhood; 6.7 percent of businesses hired one-quarter to one-half of their employees from the neighborhood. The remaining 23 percent reported that they hired fewer than one-quarter of their employees from the neighborhood. Firms in manufacturing and finance, insurance, and real estate typically belonged to lowest category of neighborhood hiring.

Recruitment

Neighborhood organizations that help residents secure employment should be aware that Grand Boulevard firms currently do not look to public-sector training programs to prepare employees, nor do they make much use of neighborhood organizations to find workers. Instead, firms in the Grand Boulevard area rely on informal methods. Three-quarters of employers reported that they recruited through word of mouth, 38.9 percent hired friends and relatives of current employees, and 36.1 percent found workers through advertisements in local newspapers.

Firms in the area reported that they made little use of established employment assistance mechanisms. Fourteen percent used employment agencies and state job services; only 8.3 percent reported that they contacted community organizations to find potential employees.

The heavy reliance on informal recruitment methods rather than formal training and placement programs is consistent with the employment experiences of Job Training Partnership Act (JTPA) participants. Retention rates of JTPA participants by small service-sector firms, like many of those in the Grand Boulevard area, are lower than those of firms in other industries (Wong and Roselius 1990). It is likely that because of the high employee turnover that characterizes the small-business sector and because of area firms' reliance on contingent workers, those businesses choose to recruit workers through the least expensive and least time-consuming methods such as word of mouth.

Education Required for Employment

A high school diploma or equivalent is required for most jobs in Grand Boulevard-area firms. With few exceptions, employers indicated that diplomas were required for machine operator, transportation, sales, and laborer positions. For craft workers, special training is typically required in addition to a high school diploma.

Service-sector firms in the Chicago metropolitan area rely more heavily than others on credentials such as a high school diploma, and on workers' appearance and communication skills (Wong and Roselius 1990). Apparently the use of these hiring criteria allows firms to differentiate between the many low-skilled job applicants interviewed for entry-level positions. This finding may explain Grand Boulevard firms' heavy reliance on minimum education requirements and raises an important question: Where can job opportunities be found for job seekers who do not possess a high school education?

Worker Training

Formal training programs play little role in preparing job seekers for employment in Grand Boulevard-area firms. Furthermore, few firms provide formal in-house training for their employees. Such training was provided by 8.6 percent of the firms, and 5.7 percent employed workers who had been trained in programs funded under JTPA. Nearly 75 percent of the firms, however, provided some sort of orientation to prepare employees for the job.

There are several reasons why small businesses provide less training per employee than larger firms (Bosworth 1989). First, operations in small businesses, particularly in retail trade and services, tend to be labor-intensive; thus the firms' training budgets are spread thinly across the workforce. Second, returns to training are diminished by the lower average levels of specialization of employees in small firms. Third, the higher rates of employee turnover in small firms reduce firms' willingness to expend resources for training. In short, training by small firms does not "anchor" employees to the firms. In a sense, training undertaken by such an employer would prepare the employee for the next job in another firm.

Firms' disincentives for training are compounded by individual employees' generally lower investments in small firms and by the frequently poorer quality of work-related education available to most inner-city residents. Together these forces result in a general underinvestment in training in the Grand Boulevard area, which places residents at a disadvantage in the labor market.

Designing Strategies for Inner-City Economic Development

Findings from surveys of neighborhood residents and area businesses challenge the notion that after decades of economic decline, disinvestment, and deepening poverty, inner-city neighborhoods such as Grand Boulevard can reverse their fortunes simply by adopting a "bootstrap" approach to revitalization. Job seekers are increasingly disconnected from emerging employment centers, and the neighborhood economy has lost its capacity to generate sufficient employment opportunities for residents. The resulting lack of employment opportunities has depressed residents' income levels until they can no longer support a high level of commercial activity, and has undermined the economic foundation of the neighborhood. A neighborhood's ability to rejuvenate itself is questionable as long as this cycle of decline continues to define the local economy.

Through its large infusion of economic development funds and supporting public policies, the EZ/EC process can be a much-needed catalyst for economic revitalization in Grand Boulevard and other neighborhoods. Next we examine the Chicago EZ/EC goals in the context of the economic situation facing Grand Boulevard residents.

EZ/EC Goals

Building on Residents' Skill Base to Develop Jobs That Pay a Livable Wage

For many job seekers living in economically distressed neighborhoods, recent work experiences and skills may be their strongest assets. Job seekers who are able to find positions that build on their skills can move up the career ladder into better-paying jobs. Those who cannot do so often accept jobs in another field or positions for which they are overqualified. The resulting mismatch between workers' skills and the skills required by the job produces labor market outcomes that are costly both for the mismatched workers and for the jobless.

Labor force-based development is one approach to building on workers' assets by identifying appropriate employment opportunities that are within reach of job seekers. Such development is unlike traditional strategies, which focus on employers' needs with the assumption that market forces will bring workers together with firms for a mutually beneficial outcome (Ranney and Betancur 1992). Instead this approach seeks (1) to build on neighborhood residents' skills and work experiences by identifying appropriate employment opportunities that are accessible to residents and (2) to target development, placement, and training activities to these jobs and locations. In other words, firms' needs are not used as a starting point in evaluating employment opportunities; rather, strategies are created in an attempt to capitalize on workers' existing skills. (For a description of the analytical tools needed to conduct labor force-based development, see Ranney and Betancur 1992; Theodore and Carlson 1997). Labor force-based development provides an opportunity to target assistance and improve its effectiveness by matching employers' needs to workers' skills.

Expansion of Job Training Services

The underinvestment in Grand Boulevard workers' education and vocational training contributes to the poor labor market preparation of many neighborhood residents. The expansion of job training services to give Grand Boulevard residents the opportunity to gain needed workplace skills could significantly enhance area job seekers' employability. It appears, however, that job training activities undertaken through the EZ/EC process are directed most appropriately at employment opportunities outside Grand Boulevard. The scarcity of employment opportunities available in the area and the employment needs and hiring strategies of neighborhood businesses reveal issues that override job-training concerns. Large-scale job training directed at employment in neighborhood firms will be needed only after the demand for skilled labor increases. Insofar as area firms request training programs for their employees, such training might better be provided through incentives for employers to provide training themselves or in conjunction with community organizations.

Another successful approach may be targeting job-training services to give job seekers greater access to growing industries, such as health care, that are located near Grand Boulevard. When combined with career counseling, such training could significantly expand employment opportunities and provide avenues for career mobility.

Strengthening Links Between Community Organizations and Businesses

Community organizations serving Grand Boulevard are looking increasingly to the neighborhood as a source of employment for local residents. However, opportunities to help job seekers find employment may be limited in the absence of outreach to residents and businesses. Both community residents and local businesses rely on informal methods of job search and worker recruitment. Job seekers rarely use employment agencies and community organizations. Similarly, neighborhood businesses rarely consult these intermediaries for referrals.

Workers and employers might be matched more successfully if community organizations were to perform such an intermediary function. In time, neighborhood businesses might come to depend on these organizations for employee referrals; job seekers might look to the organizations to direct their job search activities. Yet it is unlikely that businesses would pay for this service because most employ entry-level workers at low wages; therefore the costs of the search would exceed the benefits. Also, many employers have adopted core-contingent strategies that give them access to needed workers at low direct costs.

Although full-time employment opportunities are scarce in the Grand Boulevard area, many businesses stated that they provide part-time employment to high school students. Such employment furnishes students with modest incomes as well as job experience and an introduction to the "world of work." Yet there is evidence that job information networks in inner-city neighborhoods function poorly. As a result, students may not become aware of employment opportunities (Holzer 1987).

Survey results show that area employers rely on word-of-mouth notification, recommendations from employees, and other informal means of recruitment. Local School Councils (LSCs), which are present at all Chicago public schools, also could facilitate the flow of job information. Community organizations that work with businesses, as well as the employers themselves, could operate through LSCs to disseminate information about employment opportunities for young people.

Supporting Neighborhood Business Development

In many inner-city neighborhoods, community-based organizations are the primary influence on economic development decision making. These organizations deliver needed services, advocate on behalf of neighborhood employers, and work to attract new businesses.

However, community-based organizations' involvement in facilitating business development is full of potential pitfalls. The low success rates of new business ventures, the economic marginalization of many inner-city businesses, and the likelihood of displacing existing businesses may limit the benefits of community-initiated efforts at business development (Betancur, Bennett, and Wright 1991).

Resources must be devoted to business development efforts that meet the neighborhood residents' needs. One strategy might be to use residents' skills as a guide for development. Efforts to attract and retain business may depend on the ability of the neighborhood labor force to satisfy the businesses' labor needs. Targeting retention and attraction activities to firms that are likely to employ neighborhood residents could be a way of enticing businesses to locate in the area and provide employment opportunities for residents.

The EZ/EC process is designed to foster community-based revitalization strategies to stimulate development in inner-city neighborhoods. In the process, community planners will confront economic decline that has

204

been decades in the making. Successful revitalization strategies will demand creativity; traditional approaches have been tried, and more often than not they have failed.

Beyond the goals stated in the Chicago EZ/EC application, what should be expected from new revitalization efforts? Just as innovative strategies must emerge from residents, community organizations, and their partners, so must measurable goals and benchmarks of progress. On the eve of this historic revitalization program, processes of decline have created a bleak situation. If the EZ/EC process is deemed to be a failure after programs and policies have been tried and evaluated, a long time could pass before another large-scale federal initiative is undertaken to assist economically disadvantaged neighborhoods.

Notes

1. During a focus group discussion involving Grand Boulevard residents, several participants related work experiences that included employment in the manufacturing sector. As firms closed or relocated outside the Chicago area, opportunities for employment in this sector declined, and these workers turned to lesser-skilled and lower-paying occupations that were more readily available.

2. Research for this section was funded by the John D. And Catherine T. Mac Arthur Foundation and the Policy Research and Action Group. Tony Martin, Pamela Doan, and Kai Jackson of the Kenwood Oakland Community Organization and Dwayne Falls of the Chicago Urban League conducted the surveys of business owners and managers. Centers for New Horizons provided the results of a neighborhood survey that was used to identify area businesses.

3. The businesses surveyed were identified through a neighborhood survey and were supplemented by listing from the *Harris Directory*, the *Directory of Services*, and the *Directory of Manufacturers*. From these sources, we identified 401 businesses and divided them into five categories: (1) retail trade (200 businesses, 49.9 percent); (2) personal services and repair (86 businesses, 21.4 percent); and (3) eating and drinking establishments (68 businesses, 2.2 percent). From this list we selected a representative sample of 38 businesses and conducted interviews. The number of businesses selected for interview from each industry category matched the proportion of those business found in the area. We assumed that the practices and experiences of the interviewed firms were representative of businesses in the respective sectors in the area under study, and thus allowed us to reach conclusions about the entire list of firms. We made an exception for manufacturing firms: we contacted all nine manufacturers, and six responded. To improve the quality of responses, we conducted surveys by telephone and through face-to-face interviews with business owners or managers.

4. *Internal labor* market refers to employment opportunities within a firm; *external labor* force refers to the overall labor market.

5. In this, statement we assume that even though large firms may use contigent workers to a considerable extent, those firms on average still retain workers with a greater range of skill levels.

Chapter 8

In Their Own Words

Interviews With Participants in the Empowerment Zone Planning Process

2 interviews.

Michael Bennett and Javier Nogueras

The following interviews provide insight into the dynamics of citizen participation during the application and planning phase of the Empowerment Zone process in Chicago, and in the very early implementation. These interviews reflect both the optimism and the practical skepticism of participants, from two very different vantage points, one as a community resident and participant, the other as official city hall staff. Both have been committed to making the most of the opportunities provided by the Empowerment Zone, especially having been involved in Chicago's Empowerment Zone process from very early in the planning and application phase.

At the time of the interview, Ms. Rontos worked for an alderman whose ward is in the Pilsen/Little Village Cluster of the Empowerment Zone. Before that, she was with Pilsen Neighbors, a community organization in the same part of the zone. Ms. Marquez was Mayor Richard M. Daley's key liaison during the early stages of the process.

Because these interviews discuss the Chicago process in detail, there may be terms and acronyms familiar only to those who are or have been involved in Chicago's Empowerment Zone. The following list of definitions may be helpful.

Back of the Yards: One of the neighborhoods included in the Empowerment Zone. This area has a significant amount of industrial development.

CCC: Chicago City Council.

CHA: Chicago Housing Authority.

Chicago Association of Neighborhood Development Organizations (CANDO): A city-wide coalition of community development groups that has been active in the Empowerment Zone process in Chicago since its inception.

Clusters: The six areas that make up Chicago's Empowerment Zone and locally designated Enterprise Communities. The Empowerment Zone Clusters are the South Cluster and the Pilsen/Little Village Cluster. The New Englewood Village Cluster and the Calumet Cluster are the Enterprise Communities. The West Cluster refers to both an EZ and an EC area.

The *Community Workshop on Economic Development* (CWED): A city-wide umbrella organization for community organizations. The lead community group in the Empowerment Zone process, especially during the application phase. It also hosts the Joint Governance Council.

DCCA: The State Department of Commerce and Community Affairs.

DPD: Department of Planning and Development. The lead city agency in the Empowerment Zone process.

Eighteenth Street Development Corporation: A community development organization in the Pilsen community that has participated in the EZ process since it began.

The Empowerment Zone/Enterprise Community Coordinating Council (EZ/EC CC): The formal governing entity for Chicago's EZ and EC's. The **Interim Council** is an earlier manifestation that was primarily responsible, along with the Department of Planning and Development, for writing Chicago's winning Empowerment Zone application.

Enterprise Community (EC): In Chicago, the three Enterprise Community applicants did not receive federal designation, but the City of Chicago and the State of Illinois committed support to the applicant communities and locally designated them as ECs. They participate in the official governing structure.

The Green Line: The elevated train line that connects the heart of the West side of Chicago, including the West Cluster, with downtown and the South Cluster. Community groups saved it from demolition, and it was refurbished and reopened in 1996.

El Hogar del Nino: A child care service center, involved in programs that also offers parent training. Involved with the EZ.

The Joint Governance Council (JGC): A collective of representatives from the EZ's and EC's. Established in the spring of 1994 to promote cooperation and communication across the EZ/EC, the JGC was a place for Cluster representatives to work together on the Strategic Plan, and continues to facilitate citizen participation in the implementation of Chicago's Empowerment Zone and Enterprise Communities.

Kinzie Corridor: An industrial corridor that is part of Chicago's Empowerment Zone.

Local Initiatives Service Corporation (LISC): A national organization that funds community development.

Malcolm X: One of Chicago's two-year community colleges, located in the West Cluster.

Pilsen Neighbors: A CBO that organizes around a wide variety of local issues, including development, education, and leadership development. Geared to community mobilization.

The Resurrection Project: A Pilsen community-based organization that was an early participants in the Empowerment Zone.

Seven Key Initiatives: Also known as the Seven Strategic Initiatives, these are the organizing principles or "building blocks" for Chicago's Strategic Plan. These are: Human and Organizational Capacity, Linking Health and Human Services, Public Safety, Economic Empowerment, Development of Affordable and Accessible Housing, Building on Cultural Diversity as a Critical Asset, and Youth Futures. Together, these initiatives form a systemic, holistic approach to revitalizing Chicago's Empowerment Zone communities.

Y: The YMCA

Interview with Rosanna Marquez, Office of the Mayor
Chicago, November 28, 1995

Michael Bennett (Interviewer)
What does the term "Empowerment Zone" mean to you?

Roseanna Marquez (Interviewee)
Well, it's a little hard for me to separate what I originally viewed it as from what's actually transpired.

But I'd actually have to start with what I always viewed it as originally, and continue to: a comprehensive way of approaching community revitalization. And that's it. I distinguish that from "Enterprise Zone," which for me always was about trying to deal with the business or job creation side of community revitalization, but clearly left lacking the other equally, if not more important side: the human development side. And so more than anything else, for me, Empowerment Zone means a comprehensive approach to stimulating community revitalization.

Bennett: Do you think that's a widely-shared meaning? Do you think this meaning is shared among the people that you have to work with?

Marquez: I think it's probably a question of focus. My answer would be yes, I think everyone would view it that way. Would everyone view it as the dominant way of looking at Empowerment Zones? No, I would guess not. It's also about defining relationships, particularly between people. People—especially the residents of Empowerment Zones—and government at all levels. That's also very much an element, and I think that would be defined very differently by each participant, that is, what the nature of the relationship is. It is both of those things, and while I think everyone would agree that it's about trying to take a comprehensive, holistic view of community revitalization, others would emphasize, perhaps, other aspects about it more than I would.

Bennett: Looking at the policy—the legislation itself—in your judgement, was the original concept of Empowerment Zones a valid concept?

Marquez: As far as the community revitalization issues, the answer is yes. I thought it was a very sound approach—do it all. You cannot address community revitalization without dealing with the hard business job side of it and the soft, human, more intangible part of it. I think that was absolutely right on target.

I also think that the federal government did an absolutely brilliant job of leveraging itself with this program. I think, in design, it was nothing short of brilliant. A billion dollars nationwide is not a whole lot of money. A hundred million dollars and the attendant tax incentives really isn't a whole lot. But to dangle the promise of a share of a billion dollars worth of incentives to virtually every community in the country, as a way to try and excite them about community-based planning, was, I thought, absolutely brilliant. And to build that incentive into the legislation, that is, that there would still be offerings for non-designated communities that committed to a community-based planning process, I thought, was absolutely brilliant in design.

I think more thought could have been given about defining the kinds of relationships that the federal government expected to see created out of this process. There I think there was something lacking, or you know, additional thought that could have been given. But in design a lot of it was right on target.

I think the problems are largely with the relationship issues, and some of the process issues. I would have had some quarrel with process. One specific thing, to give communities no more than about a year to try to identify themselves, work out relationships, create a strategic plan—a real strategic plan—and the concrete steps to implement that plan was not realistic. So I think that was a flaw. I have heard that some of the original proponents of the Empowerment Zone program would have preferred a two-phased process. One that would have given planning grants, and then two years to really flesh out a viable, concrete, detailed plan, and then put those up to a competition for the more substantial incentives. That sounds right to me. It should have been done that way to give all the parties time to create the kind of structure and process and relationships that you need in the long-term to develop sound strategic plans.

Bennett: One of the critical things about the Empowerment Zone is this notion of eradicating poverty. In what way does this policy address issues of poverty?

Marquez: Probably most importantly by recognizing it. I think this is the empowerment in Empowerment Zones.

Probably the most important way is by saying or assuming up front that people have to help themselves. This is not about government at any level dictating "Here's what we're going to do, and here's how we're going to spend this money to eradicate poverty." But rather, "Here are incentives, and we want all of you, especially residents, to work together as a team, to find ways to eradicate poverty." I think this was the most important way the legislation sought to do that, and then the other things are more the nuts-and-bolts, the actual dollar stuff. You create enough incentives, offer enough resources, to start to address both sides of the eradicating poverty equation. The one part is providing jobs and economic opportunity. The other is to create populations that are ready to avail themselves of jobs and economic opportunities.

Bennett: Are there any other adjustments that you could suggest in the policy, the legislation itself, that should be communicated to the federal government?

Marquez: Yes, one more. We in Chicago always thought that as important as any of the incentives was the promise of flexibility—the "waivers issue" as a lot of people put it. The federal government expressed very good intentions. "We're going to be flexible, we're going to look at any request to be more flexible in how we administer this and other federal programs." The goodwill was there. However, nothing was set up to really address it. And so we have struggled mightily with various federal bureaucracies to have our waiver requests, our requests for greater flexibility, responded to. That was really not very well coordinated up front, and I think the federal government could have served us all well to create a structure for addressing those flexibility—waiver— issues. It's trying to do so now, but it is at the back end, and that's created a fair amount of frustration.

Bennett: Are there several different bureaucracies that you have to deal with in getting this issue resolved?

Marquez: Sure. Every federal agency is its own bureaucracy. HUD administers the program, but it's HHS dollars. But, if we're going to do a comprehensive plan, if we're really going to comprehensively attack community revitalization, that implies all sorts of other activities that draw on other federal agencies, whether it's environmental agencies, looking at brown fields clean up, or if we're looking at other HHS programs like Head Start. If you want to talk about job training programs, that implies the Department of Labor. You want to talk about education strategies, that implicates the Department of Education.

Virtually every federal agency that is, in any way, in the business of serving people or communities, is implicated in this broader effort, but they were not fully brought on board and there was no structure to coordinate that.

Bennett: That's the detail that many of us don't know. It was assumed by the general public that HUD was going to be the quarterback. So if you needed something from the Department of Education, Commerce or what have you, they would actually channel it. But not so.

Marquez: Apparently . . . well, actually not. I think at the same time that the Empowerment Zone legislation was passed, the President signed an executive order creating the Community Empowerment Board. Something housed in the vice-president's office.

So from the very beginning, I saw that as the real place to address the inter-agency coordination issues at the federal level. HUD certainly wanted to play that coordinating role, and had all the good intentions, but it's awfully hard for employees of any agency at any level of government—not just the feds—to get employees at other agencies to do something for them.

Bennett: So perhaps to ease that going forward, there needs to be not just a council but a set of guidelines enabling each agency, within some parameters, to provide waivers.

Marquez: Well, guidelines . . . I don't want to infer more bureaucracy, more rules and guidelines. I think what it really needed was a structure, and that may have just been creating some inter-agency task force with a very strong hand, preferably someone from the White House, who gets the word down from on high. And that's it. "This is important to us. We want to see this succeed. You need to be flexible." When a waiver request, for example, comes in, the presumption should be the feds want to grant the waiver. I think that's what it really needed; I mean, a structure. Just a task force, inter-agency, some forum where these issues could be discussed among all the federal agencies. But more importantly, the word from on high.

Bennett: I've heard the lack of structure inherent in the policy described as one of its weaknesses; not at the federal level, but at least other levels. In the past there's been criticism that there was too much structure passed down in certain legislation. Do you have any ideas around what that happy medium might be, and what areas should have more structure, and what areas there might remain this flexibility?

Marquez: Well, it's a much broader issue than just Empowerment Zones. You're really talking about the relationship among various levels of government: federal, state and local. Each level of government, I think, has its own distinct responsibilities. And we ought to recognize that, and recognize that very clearly.

At the heart of the happy medium, I think, is a clear understanding of what the responsibilities are of each level of government. If you do that, and then let each level of government carry out its responsibilities, you can start to minimize the red tape. For example, I think there would be no question that the federal government is in charge of national defense. And so you let them do it, and the local and state governments have no business there. That's an easy one. Public safety, on the other hand, I think is very clearly a local government issue. I mean, you let local governments decide how they want to address the issue, from how many policemen they need, to how they want the force deployed and how they structure themselves to what their policies are. And that's solely a local issue.

What we're starting to see is all levels of government getting involved in all kinds of activities, and that includes things like job training, education, various social services. And I think, at the heart of the happy medium is a clear articulation. Local governments, for example, "you are principally about providing basic services to your residents". And that includes police; that includes education. I think education is largely a local issue, not a federal issue. The same for job training. You know, what kind of training you need varies wildly; depending on what the job may be, what the regional or local economy is.

I think many things are best dealt with at the local level. You're closest to the people, you're closest to the needs. The authority ought to go directly to the level of government that's closest to that responsibility. Recognize that, and then, with just some basic guidelines, allow local governments to do what they have to do. I want to make that more concrete because that sounds very abstract. The problem you get is you have federal agencies who believe they're charged with overseeing all sorts of broad policy areas, whether or not they really, truly are at the national interest or best coordinated on a national level. And agencies develop all sorts of legislation, or Congress develops legislation and all sorts of rules and regulations for them. And then states, in turn, feel they have the very same sets of responsibilities and they create their own sets of rules and regulations. And then local government, as well, feels primarily responsible and it creates its own sets of guidelines and rules and regulations.

If you recognize certain functions are best left at the local government level, then the federal government's only business should be to make sure that whatever dollars it's investing are spent well. And that may only be about back end audits. You know, "Local governments, you're in charge of job training, and we're going to give you some money to do it. We want to make sure you spend it well.

So go off, do what you think you have to, and then afterwards, tell us how you spent the money, and then we'll decide,"we may want you to repay some of the money. If you abused anything, we're certainly going to want some of the money back." And that's a very broad view of things, but that's the idea, I think.

Bennett: It seems the problem with that is that when this Empowerment Zone thing was established, it was nebulous as to how the relationships should be. They didn't give enough time for relationships to form, but neither did they define what these relationships might look like, other than that they should be "bottoms-up", whatever that means...

Marquez: Right.

Bennett: So, the question I keep asking is if they had written into the legislation more guidelines or stricter notions of how this thing ought to operate, like "maximum feasible participation" in the sixties, there would have been a backlash against that, too, right?

Marquez: Sure.

Bennett: So, as a policy person, the question is, how do you work this out? Is there any happy medium, or do you just see how things fly and try to give feedback to the government how this operates, and see if they can make adjustments next time around?

Marquez: Well, you're right, there's always a tension, right? I mean, give us broad flexibility and leeway to do whatever we want, but then again, give us some guidelines so we're not all flopping around on this stuff. We're all schizophrenic about that. I think, if we ask for a certain responsibility, we've got to be prepared to carry it out.

So we really want that flexibility. Again, I think in defining relationships, I think we've got to be prepared to hash it out. My real quarrel with the federal government—with the legislation—is really more about words than the absence of specific guidelines. I think words like "bottom-up" and "empowerment" ended up being defined by a lot of parties in so many different ways. For many, for some of the community people that we worked with, it meant a hundred percent of delegation of power to community residents and groups. I don't think it was ever supposed to be that, but the terms "empowerment" and "bottom-up" were used for a long time as clubs with local government to try and dictate the nature of the relationship. I don't think it was ever supposed to be about a hundred percent one way or the other. But terms like "bottom-up," "community-driven," "empowerment," I think will end up lending themselves to that kind of abuse.

So my problem really ends up being more with words. I would have preferred legislation that said you have to work in a "partnership"; you have to work "together"; all parties have "responsibilities". My problem really is more with that; it's words, and the use of the words, the selection of words like "bottom-up" and "empowerment", rather than partnership, etc.

Bennett: That's something that can be fixed in the next round.

Marquez: If there's ever a next round.

Bennett: Well, let's move quickly to the processes that are laid out in the legislation, and we'll talk first about the planning process. We can talk about that, because that has happened. We can speculate a little bit about the implementation process, and then we'll think a little bit about what the evaluation process should look like. How would you define your roles and responsibilities in the planning process?

Marquez: My role personally as opposed to the city's role, was very much what I would call that of a facilitator and a coordinator. My role was as the Mayor's Office point person. My view of the mayor's office always is, in all circumstances, that we act essentially as glue to bind city agencies. To help bind city government to the residents it's supposed to serve. So I worked among the departments. That means getting departments on board, making sure everybody is seeing eye-to-eye. If it means facilitating relationships with others outside the city, I always view my role that way in the mayor's office, and that's how I viewed my role here.

Bennett: How would you describe the dynamics between and among various government bodies that operated in the planning process, and the community technical assistance providers and the residents?

Marquez: This is a broad question.

Bennett: Well, the thing I think we know the least about in our project right now, is what roles other government agencies- other levels of government- played, particularly the state and the county, if any, in the planning process.

Marquez: All right. Well, I'll say first, formally, both the state and the county were represented on the Coordinating Council that developed the plan, and selected the initial boundaries for the Empowerment Zone areas.

Formally, they were included. The state was represented by a fairly senior official in the Department of Public Aid. He was terrific in terms of spending his time, lending his thoughtfulness and intelligence. And, given that he was from a state agency and not from the governor's office, especially, he actually did a remarkable job of bringing to the table some of the thoughts and some of the resources of the state and other state agencies. I can't speak highly enough of his contributions, and I think that had a lot to do with the person involved, but I also have to say that probably reflects some commitment on the part of the state itself, just generally.

The state was also represented by one or two officials of DCCA , a much less visible, active role. I would really credit the IDPA representative with what I thought was a pretty good relationship with the state in the process. The county was also represented, by someone who spent a fair amount of time on this and was always very cooperative.

Bennett: And how would you, in your own terms, paint a picture of the dynamics over the period of time this planning process was going on?

Marquez: I don't know how else to put this. The dynamics from the period where the city geared up to put together an application, until it was submitted—and really for some months after that, before designation on December 21 of last year—I don't know how else to characterize the dynamics but as almost always involving a power struggle at some level. There was substantive work done, to be sure, but virtually all of it, certainly what was done by the Coordinating Council in its meetings, was always permeated with the essential issue of who was going to control this thing. And that means how the money gets spent, which projects get funded. After a while, even how the resources got allocated among the clusters. So that dynamic was there. There was no way of getting around that.

Having said that, there was a lot of substantive work that tended to be done a little bit more at committee levels, as we tried to hash out these seven key initiatives. And the dynamic there—when we got to substance the dynamic was pretty good.

There are a lot of very good, thoughtful people with very different perspectives. Some pretty good, open minds. The dynamic, when it came to substance about anything but governance and control was pretty good; pretty cooperative. A little unfocused, I think. I think this plan still needs a lot of work. Basically good, but above all else, I think the dynamic from the beginning of '94 to the end of '94 was about defining "bottom-up" and "empowerment."

Bennett: When we look at Congress, or even the state house, we can kind of pin labels on people and almost predict how they might behave in a struggle. Was the same true in this? Did everyone fill their predicted roles?

Marquez: That's a good question. I have to think about that a little bit. The flip answer that I want to give is yeah, pretty much. But having said that, again, there were a lot of very thoughtful people involved. So it's not as though you could draw a line in a room and all the community representatives behaved this way and all the government people behaved that way. That's not really true. There are a lot of very thoughtful people involved. So what I think you had was, if you had to draw lines, you would have predominantly more community people on this side and predominantly government people on the other side. But in the middle you actually had some people talking to each other. Again, the city is full of some well-meaning, thoughtful people who, more than anything else, wanted to get a job done. And that included people on both sides, I think.

Bennett: What adjustments need to be made in the planning process, from your vantage point?

Marquez: Two things: One, we should be given more time. It is hard to develop comprehensive plans in so short a time period. I think that was one of the biggest challenges we had, but I don't know if I would do this any differently in the end. It's especially hard to do a comprehensive plan when you're picking pieces of different communities. If you look at the way we put together our map, what we really did is we took a dozen or so proposals that had good ideas, and found a way to mix and match them all together. And to force twelve sets of people and twelve sets of plans to hash it all out, I think, was an impossible task. It might have been easier to just pick off the one or two or three best ones, and just said "We are fully behind this vision, and we're going to develop implementing plans and flesh this out."

That would have been easier in the time frame, no doubt about it. But in the end, I'm not sure that's the way I would have liked to have done it. Would I have changed that? I'm not sure. There's something to be said for forcing the dynamic of bringing people together, who don't usually work together, with these twelve different proposals. There's something to be said for forcing that dynamic, but if you're going to do it, you need a lot more time than we had.

The other one is, difficult and painful though it may have been, I think we should have resolved the governance issue at the very beginning; gotten it out of the way. Because it ended up, in a lot of ways, poisoning a lot of the subsequent time spent. We should have just gotten it out of the way. Who knows how that really would have played out, but letting that discussion drag on for as long as it did became a major distraction in this effort.

Bennett: I think most observers would say that it was simply remarkable that this city, with all of the players at least that were supporting and involved, came up with the kind of plan that they did at all.

Marquez: It was an incredible accomplishment, and reflects the fact, more than anything else, that no matter what the issues were, you had a room full of very dedicated, thoughtful people who were absolutely committed. "We may have knock-down drag-outs, but we're coming back into this room. We're going to hash this out. This is too important. We've got to get this done". And it's especially because of that we were able to put something together.

Bennett: Some would argue that this time frame was helpful in that regard. That if there was a longer time frame, there would have been much more bickering, in a sense, and what helped to bring people together was the fact that there was this money out there. "We've got this period of time to get the act together, so let's go to it".

Marquez: I think that's valid. It accomplished that. No doubt. I think it was at the expense of a real set of plans. And so that goes back to one of the major changes that would have helped—to do a two-step process. To have a planning grant phase. Let the parties hash out that stuff in a short time frame, enough to put together a basic outline of a plan, which is essentially what we did, with a little more flesh on the bones. And then spend the longer time doing the more substantive competition, forcing people to do the strategic plans and not fight for the hundred million or the tax credits.

Bennett: Where it really gets to a bridge issue is the government structure. It's partially related to the planning process, but at this point it's related to the implementation stages—kind of a bridge between these two discussions.

If you look at the government structure that Chicago selected, what were the dynamics around that? What were the styles and levels of negotiations and who had a role in developing it? Did the feds have anything to say about what we ended up with?

Marquez: No, not really. The legislation, other than using some of the terms that it did —"empowerment", "bottom-up"—was pretty silent about what would be an acceptable structure. Which isn't to say that parties didn't go to the feds, nevertheless, to try and get them engaged in that discussion. But no, it was really a local issue; pretty appropriately so.

How did it all get worked out, and on what levels? I think that at all times, there were several levels of discussions. Most formally there were the clusters and there was the city. And it was very much a classic negotiation. Each went off among themselves and worked out their negotiating positions and came together and try to hash it out. But it was a fairly difficult, if not, impossible negotiation. And so I think that gave rise to some other levels of discussion.

Again, you have a fair number of fairly thoughtful people who would actually try and think through where the common ground was. Some of that was accomplished in the bigger rooms, but not much. The rhetoric was pretty polarized on all sides in the more formal setting.

So at a second level, I think there were some people on both sides who tried to find the common ground; who tried to find something that could be built on. And so in the end, when it comes down to the formal structure, most of the key structural issues, if not all the key structural issues, came to a vote. And it turns out there was some fairly common ground.

For example, I think everyone agreed that a majority of the people serving on the Coordinating Council should be people who live in these areas. That we needed to do a better job of trying to engage the private and other sectors. So just in terms of the structure, it ultimately came to a vote. And there is a fair amount of common ground on the structure. I think the real fight, and one never amicably resolved, was who gets to pick the members. And the only way that got resolved finally was the city and the City Council just did what they felt they had to do, and it was to bring the issue to a head, take it to the City Council.

Bennett: You couldn't really get a sense of where this thing was going and what the major bones of contention were. Except who chooses. Were there other things?

Marquez: Well, I'll add to that. I'm remembering a little bit more now and would add this as well. The key seemed to be who chooses, but the real key issue and the reason why the discussion got more complex, was that it really was about control over resources. And so that includes all the structural issues.

How do you try and stack the votes in your favor as much as possible? How do you divide up the pie among community residents? And then within the clusters, do they all have equal say? And what about those EC's that weren't designated, who still want to feel a part of the process? All of that is about trying to line up your votes, and you can try and slice that issue all sorts of ways. But that permeates the structural issue.

Again, a lot of this was about control and power, and it was also about what you're controlling in this. Some of the proposals, for example, would have authorized this Coordinating Council to have all power over land use issues in the Empowerment Zone. Some proposals wanted to create, essentially, a self-sustaining entity with bonding authority with power of veto, power to create land trusts of public property. It was more complex. It wasn't just a who controls and who picks, it's what's being controlled and picked here. And how do we use this? Again, trying to pick from various proposals, how do we use this structure to try to dictate to business what it does, to make business more responsive? Can we use this to hold up the tax credits until businesses do more community hiring, or contribute to service provision in these areas?

All of that was a part of the governance discussion as well. And so throw all that in and it starts to get fairly complicated. What's the number, who picks, what are they really controlling? What's the role of the City Council? There really were three key parties in this discussion: city government, the administration, community—however you want to define that, it's not, obviously, a monolith—and the City Council, which only toward the end started openly asserting itself. But there was a whole three-way discussion going on here.

Bennett: Now, where did all these proposals emerge? From the clusters themselves?

Marquez: Yes. Well, I think through the Joint Governance Council. In the early proposals, clusters weren't each proposing different things. They had their act together and different things got floated at different times. Although again, toward the end it was clear that the different clusters had different views on some of these issues, or were more willing to give on some issues than on others. But the proposals were always presented as a proposal of the Joint Governance Council of all three clusters; all six clusters counting the EC's.

Bennett: One issue that's fascinating to me is the role of City Council individuals. The thing that struck me was that in some instances a City Council person—the elected representative of an area— actually saw the cluster in that area wearing the leadership, and therefore as opposition.

Marquez: That's very threatening! I think that was always going on. I'm doing some speculating because I didn't deal with the aldermen as much as the planning department did, but it was quite clear. To some extent, I think this is a legitimate issue, that of who really represents the people who live in this area. And you had two very opposing views. You now had clusters asserting themselves as the chosen elected—they had an election process—as the elected spokes people for their community, period. And you had the aldermen saying "Well, you know what? That's exactly what we are." And so that was always-- you can say the aldermen felt threatened. I don't know how you would say the clusters felt about their aldermen, but there were clearly very opposing sets of views.

If it came right down to it, aldermen were never going to cede that authority to the clusters. They'll work with them, sure, for all sorts of good reasons. But when it comes right down to it, this treads on traditional aldermanic domain, and this goes to the heart of what aldermen view as their domain. It includes power over land-use issues and resources. On some things aldermen will act in the broader interest of the city. But stuff like this: land, resources, and social services go at the heart of what aldermen believe their responsibilities are about, and they're not about to give those up to anybody.

Bennett: We do have to look forward to the fun of implementation, and as we talk about that, what structures have been put in place at the government level, and at the community level, to facilitate the implementation of the strategic plan?

Marquez: I can talk about the city level; I'm less sure what's been going on at the community level over the last few months. A couple of things—right after designation, the mayor felt it was very important to have a full time project manager to oversee this, so the city recently hired a full-time project manager for the Empowerment Zone to replace the person who served in the interim.

The new project manager had served previously as the federal government's near full-time liaison to Chicago's Empowerment Zone. I can't speak highly enough of his talent and his dedication. So I personally-

Bennett: Is he from Chicago—a Chicagoan?

Marquez: Originally, although he's been away, I think, for sometime... He's terrific. And so one key structural element was finding the best talented go-getting person who will help pull all these pieces together, and the new project manager is terrific, so that's one. The second is to see through the appointment of the permanent Coordinating Council. I would really like to think with all the governance issues behind us, whatever feelings people may have had about that, that the new Coordinating Council will have fresh legs, fresh energy, a fresh view. There's some continuity; I think there's about a dozen or so people who are carry-overs from the interim Coordinating Council, but with some fresh blood and energy to be prepared to start moving forward. I consider that to be a very important structural element.

After a couple of years, I honestly think a lot of people burned out some on this experience, and so leaving the major fight behind us and bringing in some new, fresh people should help a lot, I hope. Government structurally remains a priority issue for us; that's less a structural thing than it is a continuing dictate, if you will, from the highest levels of city government that this is an important initiative, and therefore, all city departments ought to continue to cooperate. I'd say the city departments were actually very good in this exercise. I shouldn't sound surprised. But it's good. It's good! We had about six or seven departments that were always there; really, cooperated in a good way: brought their resources; were creative in thinking about how to do all this; you know, weren't just about here's their piece of it, or how do they get some of the hundred million to implement their program. And I think that was a reflection; from the very beginning, a reflection of this administration, that this was a pretty high priority, and something that we hammered at all the time. And so that structure has been there since the beginning. It's still there.

City departments know this is a very, very important initiative, and that their continuing active cooperation is important. And they'll do that. The other thing we've done, structurally, on the government side, is to bring in, some of the other agencies. Non-city government agencies that really play a key role are coming in, such as the school board, which had not been involved, the CHA—whose residents comprise a pretty sizeable percentage of the zone residents—are now a part of this Coordinating Council. That's another part that we thought had been missing.

Bennett: I've found it important to stop talking about The City, or The Community, as though each person who works for the city behaves and thinks in the same way. Instead, I prefer to talk more about who in the city or community or wherever.

Marquez: Absolutely.

Bennett: So if we think about the Coordinating Council, for example, and the advice to the mayor...

Marquez: And a lot of people who advise the mayor.

Bennett: Yeah. If you think about who really makes the decisions about the Empowerment Zone in the previous stage, was it the collaboration of departments that kind of got together and made these decisions, or was it more like three or four people who advised the mayor, mostly to the outside issues?

Marquez: Yes, I could name a few key people, especially looking backwards. Things are evolving, so names will change, but there clearly were just a couple people who were much more involved in advising the mayor. And directing the efforts of others, sure.

Bennett: And as you think about the kind of structures that are in place, are any of these new or innovative? Are there any innovations that have come out of this in terms of structures in place and limitations?

Marquez: New to the Empowerment Zone initiative- nothing is brand new. This Coordinating Council is a very different creature than you've seen in the past, although I could probably draw its roots in various places. They're not unlike the CCC, only they're making recommendations about a whole lot more than just land use, which is what the CCC is about. Project managers, you know, full-time project managers; this administration has been making use of them for some time. That's a good question: Is there anything that is just brand-spanking-new about this?

Bennett: Yeah.

Marquez: No.

Bennett: Okay. We'll keep looking, because there may be. This supposed to be an opportunity, either at the community level or government level, to be some new kinds of things, especially in structures. And maybe in the programs.

Marquez: I think that is a good way of putting it. Now, I would guess at the community level that's incredibly true. The cluster structure itself. I thought that was an innovative structure. I mean, it was disciplined structure . . . formal. That fact alone I thought was pretty interesting. I think that out of this effort at the community level, we're seeing new organizations emerge.But no, anything brand-spanking-new structurally? I don't think so. I will say this though, and this is not a structural thing—a lot of people aren't used to working together.

Bennett: Yeah.

Marquez: Working together—that was innovative, but it had its pitfalls. This approach of taking the best of different proposals instead of dealing with the same cast of characters here and cast of characters there. The city could easily have chosen groups or areas where we already worked with these people, where the relationships are worked out, and we could just get on with the business of it. We didn't do that. If there's anything innovative it was that. It was about taking what we thought were the best elements of everything out there, even though it involved a whole new different set of people and organizations, and maybe even organizations we haven't worked with or worked well with in the past, and said, "Damn it, we're going to do it. We're going to make ourselves all go though this exercise." And I gotta give the city- I gotta give us some credit, a lot of credit, for that.

Bennett: The idea is that this implementation process would involve all levels of people in a broad community. We know that the city will have some role, both functional and non. From your vantage point, which ways should the rank and file community residents have input?

Marquez: They should like crazy, but we've all—and by we, now, I mean all of city government and the clusters—we have all done a bad job of getting the word out and recruiting. It gets a little unwieldy to have two hundred thousand people in the room. So it's a question of how you make it happen. But we've got to be able to create a better pipeline than we have, for getting more voices. Because at this point, I think it's the same on both sides.

On the community side we're probably talking about one, maybe two hundred people. But beyond that the word isn't out. People barely know it exits. And you know, they may find out it exists if a nice store opens up next to them or they find a nice day care center. That would actually be pretty significant where a working- a single mother could leave her kids so she could work. But beyond those couple hundred people or so, my guess is that the word Empowerment Zone doesn't mean anything to a hundred ninety-nine thousand five hundred people living in these areas, and that's not good. And we've got to find some way to get them more engaged, involved; and recruit talent and not allow this to be self-perpetuating among the same sets of players on any side of the equation. I don't have the answer to that. We're not doing it yet. We're not doing it well. And we've got to do it—all of us—better.

Bennett: That's something I think we want to see, and if anybody's done it better around the country, which I doubt, try to get that out so people are conscious of it.

Marquez: Right. Well, we tried the public meeting thing, but how do you get people to show up? How do you get people who otherwise don't ascribe anything to the term Empowerment Zone to decide it's worth a couple hours of their time to come to a meeting and find out what this is about? Setting up the meetings and sending out the flyers wasn't doing it.

Bennett: Given that, you know, there will be some major successes as a result of Empowerment Zones. In which ways do you think the effectiveness of Empowerment Zones should be measured?

Marquez: Some of it is easy, and should be used. The statistical information, like employment rates, income levels and the population in these areas. If these become attractive areas more people will come and live in them. Also retention. Some of it starts to get pretty interesting. No one wants to gentrify these places so that the very people that who are supposed to benefit get pushed out. I mean, if they want to move out of their own choice—move up and on, fine—but I'd be interested in something like that.

Again, a lot of the statistical data is easy. The graduation rates of the schools. I mean, we can come up with a dozen statistical indexes. But how do you measure, really, whether the quality of someone's life has improved? And I don't know the answer to that. These days I'm struggling with exactly this issue with the CHA.

That's something I'm much more involved in these days. How do you measure changes in the quality of life for zone residents? Some of it—surveys, I mean, that sounds goofy, but maybe not too—feedback-direct feedback is the best way. How do you get direct feedback? Well, a well-crafted survey would help. How do you get a good response rate? That's another challenge. But you know, direct feedback is terribly important. I would love to see—this is statistical, but—for me a measure of a community's strength is how involved and engaged its residents are. I don't know how you count that up, but how many of the residents are actually involved in something, whether it's the block club or a community policing effort, or whatever you call it?

Bennett: So maybe do a baseline survey and one year, two years, three years out do more surveys and selective interviews to figure out what made the difference, if anything. Was it Empowerment Zone activities or something more? It's usually something broader. But we're interested in trying to keep track of this. So quality of life issues, extension of involvement, engagement and levels of engagement. In what kind of universe do you think it's fair to look at Empowerment Zone process?

Marquez: The first thing that jumped out of my head was annually, certainly no less frequently. More frequently; every six months? You could break it down. Some of the statistical data is easy enough to compile, so maybe do that every six months or so. The number of jobs, any business move-ins, income levels. Statistical analyses twice a year sounds more doable to me than the less tangible stuff: the surveys, the interviews, the levels of involvement. Annually? I don't want to weigh this thing down to much with, well, evaluation-related processes.

Bennett: Now, does the city itself have any evaluation process in place, in terms of measuring some of these things? For example, I heard that some city department had done a survey of some fifteen hundred businesses in the zone.

Marquez: Yes. Continental Bank, now Bank of America, had very early on, with some city help, sent out a survey to all businesses with annual revenues of a million dollars or more in the zones, that among other things asked if we made these incentives available to you—tax incentives and this and that— How many additional people do you think you would hire? Which was kind of interesting. My memory is a little rusty on the numbers, but I think we got about a fifteen percent response rate, and the number of job commitments numbered around fourteen hundred or so. That was interesting.

More importantly, the Department of Planning and Development, shortly after designation, put together a business base—it actually went knocking on doors, sent out surveys, tried to get in touch with virtually every business, mid-sized or larger. I don't know what the threshold was- business located within the zone. And out of that they created baseline data, current size, workforce, information like that. I don't know just what they've done by way of follow-up. The survey was done for a number of reasons: get the word out, start doing some marketing. But one purpose as well was to create that baseline of information with respect to just business activity in the zone. That's the only one that I'm aware of that's in place.

Bennett: Flipping a little bit back to an earlier question, there was a decision made—and this is another place where people want to give this plan trophies, you know, as remarkable—but there had to be some hard decisions made about where industry was going to be included in the zone, as opposed to residential areas.

Marquez: You're talking about the map issue.

Bennett: Which people were saying was looking into the future towards the implementation. And saying "If we're going to find a job, we have to have this thing where we can leverage existing jobs and industry. So we're going to have to sacrifice some residential areas and human development types of things, for the Back of the Yards, or someplace where there's industrial development." Do you remember any of that discussion?

Marquez: Oh, very well, actually. I thought this was one of the more fascinating, productive discussions. Now, this is the interim Coordinating Council that existed before the clusters were formally involved, so it's a different set of people now.

The mayor had initially appointed a thirty person council in charge of doing the map, and after the map was selected, the clusters asserted themselves and the Council was reconfigured to give them half the seats.But having said that, still, there is some community representation on this first Coordinating Council.

Let me take a step back and make sure this is clear. You know we had set up a selection process up front; essentially an RFP, which drew thirty-three proposals, largely from community, almost exclusively community-based proposals. The thirty-three proposals were largely from community-based organizations, and their emphasis was very much on capturing people. Almost without exception, they were about people. And so the areas tended to be almost exclusively residential, which made a very tough issue for us; for this council.

We wrestled very quickly with the question "Can we go outside the proposed boundaries?" If you take a map and put all the territory the proposals covered, can we go outside those boundaries to capture what we think are economic activities; those industrial corridors? And a very early call was "We have no choice." If all you do is capture need without opportunity, this thing is going to fail. That was a difficult discussion. But, you know, we got through it. DPD had its various divisions do presentations on economic, industrial areas of opportunity. Then we scored, if you will, these thirty-three proposals, found a dozen or so that got a passing score. So we know now this is the universe of areas we're looking at. It was still huge. If I remember, the population of just those twelve proposals still was around a million. It was huge; we still had to do major carving. It was not going to be too popular to do a lot of that carving to make room for economic opportunity. But we were prepared to do it.

We needed to see industrial corridors. We now needed state enterprise zones, whatever; what's out there had to be linked to all of these residential areas, because there had to be no more than three non-contiguous areas, etc. And so that presentation was done. It may have taken two different meetings. And it had all sort of overlays, you know, "Here's what we've got here; we've got Back of the Yards; and here's what the land and vacancy situation is. Here's where we think there may be some prospects; businesses thinking of expansion may be moving in." Same thing with the Kinzie Corridor, same thing with- we went through virtually all of those sorts of opportunities that were adjacent to any of the residential areas that we were looking at.

And then with that, it just became the carving exercise. You know, how do you take those proposals and try both to capture two hundred thousand people in need, but also link them up with economic opportunity? And I remember arguments made on that. By then, by the time that you get to the decision that you're going to do this, it's just the exercise of making the judgements about where we think the best opportunities lie. There's one more thing you have to relate in this, though.

This is funny from my perspective. Virtually everybody involved in the process from the very beginning, on all sides—community, some of the citywide organizations—CANDO, LISC, CWED, citywide agencies—individually we all had made the judgement that the CTA's Green Line had to be a key part of this. But for awhile, no one came out and said that. So it almost seemed like an epic struggle over something that we all agreed about. Remember, at some of the meetings, community folks say "You practically have a fiduciary obligation to revolve the zone—people and economic opportunity, whatever, around the green line." And your different parties were campaigning like mad. But we had all been thinking that, so making that decision was not that difficult.

And in pulling together the residents, the residential areas, the economic opportunities, the one dominant geographic pattern you see is the CTA's Green Line. And that was not an accident.

Bennett: Well, thank you very much.

Marquez: My pleasure. I don't know if I said anything differently, or if I said anything new, but that's certainly the way I see it.

Interview with Sherry Rontos
Chicago December 4, 1995

Javier Nogueras (interviewer): What does the Empowerment Zone mean to you?

Sherry Rontos (interviewee): I think it means many things, ranging from headaches, heartaches, to the hundred million dollar social service block grant funding. The Empowerment Zone hasn't reached the stage of empowering the people yet, but I think it has given us a bridge and a reason to come together around the table.

The Empowerment Zone, to me, is getting people together that might not have the opportunity or desire to work together towards one common goal.

Nogueras: Can you give an example of people who have come together?

Rontos: OK. Use the Pilsen/Little Village Cluster. The different entities—Resurrection, 18th Street Development, Pilsen Neighbors, El Hogar, the YMCA, and others—all these different groups might not have worked together. Some of them couldn't stand each other, but they all came together and they had to work toward a common goal, and that was for the betterment of the community and to get the Zone in this area.

On the government's side, I think the aldermen kind of stayed back, because I don't think that local government understood from the beginning what their role was in this. It was also an understanding that this, as the Empowerment Zone, was supposed to be from the bottoms-up, but where does your local government fit into a bottoms-up process? Because they are people, they're people that live within the community. And also, they're people that influence change. But where do they fit in the Empowerment Zone? I don't think there has been a clearly defined role yet for them within the Empowerment Zone. I think that's very important, that it's an issue that needs to be looked at, and maybe that could be part of re-inventing government.

Nogueras: Do you think "Empowerment Zone" means the same thing to others?

Rontos: I think when you talk about headaches, heartaches and people that disagree coming together, I think that's where people would agree. It means different things to everybody, and I think that all of us are looking to see that this makes changes. If you asked everybody individually what's it mean to them, they would take their personal slant—whatever is in their self-interest.

To me, personally, I'm in the middle of the Empowerment Zone. I don't necessarily know what it means to me as a person yet, or as a person that lives in the Pilsen/Little Village Cluster of the Empowerment Zone. I don't understand yet what benefit I will get from it. So as an individual, I don't understand it. From a community aspect I understand, and from a government aspect I understand. But as a community resident?

What does it mean to me? Am I getting a tax break? No. Am I getting anything from it? No. Am I personally going to benefit from it? No. But as for the community, I understand what it means to not-for-profits. I understand what it means for government. I understand what it means as far as policy. And that might be a trickle down effect to me. But I'm not going to feel that right away, and that's not hitting my pocketbook, and that's not affecting me immediately. And the policies that are changed might not even affect me at all. So I think you'll have different perspectives on it.

Nogueras: In your judgement, was the original concept of the Empowerment Zone a valid concept, as outlined in the policy?

Rontos: I think that the original concept of the Empowerment Zone was valid. I think it was good and idealistic. You want to have high ideals, so at least you can shoot for the middle. (laughter) Hopefully you shoot high and you score center. I'm hoping that will happen.

But I think also, it shows that the government has been listening to the people. Because those concepts came out of hearing what people have to say, people were saying "Hey, you know, we've got to fight poverty. We've got to do it from the bottoms-up. We know what the problems are in our neighborhoods. You've got to come talk to the people in the street." And so I think that, yes, this came out of listening to the people.

Nogueras: Were the problems that policy sought to address the right problems?

Rontos: I think a lot of them were the right problems... I hate using it as 'Were these the right problems?" I think that's a bad term...

Nogueras: Why is that?

Rontos: Because it sounds so negative—'Are these the right problems?" One of the things that wasn't in there was immigration. Now, is that a "right" problem. You know, there's so many other kinds of things that we could talk about. Are those the right problems? And not only that, you've got to remember, too, that if we just looked and said "Oh my God, look at all the problems we have", then you get so depressed you don't want to get out of bed in the morning. So, I think saying "Are these the right problems" is kind of a strange question. And seeing these as problems. Yes, they're problems, but also if you turn them around they can be real positive things. Take the issue of housing for example. You don't have to necessarily see housing as a problem. Housing can be good as well.

When you look at housing, are you looking at bricks and mortar? Are you looking at all the positive things that happen in housing in our cultures? How Mexican Americans have family living together? Why we're overcrowded? We're overcrowded; that's not necessarily a bad thing. That's a good thing, too. We're overcrowded—that's a problem, yes, it's a problem—but at the same time, we care so much about the family, that we're overcrowded because we live together. So is that the right problem? Is that a problem? Something to look at.

Nogueras: Were the solutions urged by the policy the right solutions?

Rontos: I think the right solutions will be the solutions that come. I don't know necessarily if the solutions urged by the policy will be the right solutions. I know that the right solutions will come from the bottoms-up if given a chance. And will only come if it's both government and people working together. People shouldn't see the government as being necessarily wrong about their solutions, and government shouldn't be threatened by the solutions of people. They should see the Empowerment Zone as an equal playing field where they both can come to the table with ideas and say `OK, this is on the table. What do you think?" That should be the place where we can feel safe and empowered. So it should become the Safe Zone! (laughs)

Nogueras: Safe Zone! (laughs)

Rontos: Instead of the Empowerment Zone. Think about it. Think about how empowering that would be for people to feel that they were on the same level as government. And at the same time, how frightening for government to feel that it's on the same level as people.

So how does government feel empowered in a bottoms-up process? I think they should just get over their fear and just feel as one of the players that are coming to the table, not feel necessarily empowered or not empowered, but just as a player at the table. The regular people should feel empowered because they haven't been able to be at the table in such a manner. But it should be in way where people could share ideas for solutions, not be afraid to be idealistic. If everybody was sitting around sharing ideas, we'd build better relationships and a better way of looking at solutions together.

Nogueras: In what ways does the policy address the issues of poverty?

Rontos: I think that it pushes for the alleviation of poverty. I don't think that poverty is good, but I think there's a lot we can learn from poverty.

I think what else is interesting is that when a child is poor and they grow up, they don't know they were poor until somebody told them they were poor. I remember the first time I read in a history book that the neighborhood I lived in was a ghetto. I was angry because I said "Wait a minute, I don't live in the ghetto." When people talk about poverty, I think often that's negative connotations with poverty. I think we need to take what's good out of there, and to alleviate poverty in a positive manner. I don't have the answer for that. I just know that there has to be an alleviation of poverty, but I think we have to take the lessons that we learn from poverty, take those and turn that around or bring it out some way. Because there are a lot of people who will tell you that "When I was poor, I was happy." So, okay, when you were poor, what made you happy? And even people that were poor that might have liked beans and rice and tortillas, will still eat beans and rice and tortillas, or potatoes and carrots. Even though they have money to eat other things. So, there's just certain things that you never give up, and there's certain ideals you have, too. I think that goes along with poverty.

But in the legislation and justice view—issues of poverty—I think it's a White Man's definition.

Nogueras: Elaborate on that.

Rontos: The people who wrote this and who are addressing poverty probably never knew what it was like to be poor; probably never felt what it was like to go hungry to school, and probably never will. They will never know what it was like to be homeless. I don't necessarily think that you have to have that experience, but at the same time, I think if you're in an ivory tower and you're writing policy, that you can't feel it. You don't know it. So by the way it was written, it was really written like a White Man's poverty policy. (laughs)

When I say, "White Man's policy," I'm not trying to be racist. It comes from the people I have experienced and met through the Empowerment Zone process who have dealt with policy issues.

What I'm trying to get across is poor people have ideas about alleviating poverty and some are good and some are bad. We need to give them support and guidance to structure the good ideas into policy. When I say "we" I include planners, agencies, and government. None of this is easy, and it will be time-consuming. But the Empowerment Zone is supposed to create changes from the bottom-up.

Nogueras: What adjustments should be made in the policy, in the legislation?

Rontos: I think we'll learn that as we go along. At this point, we haven't put much into action yet. So how are we going to know what adjustments to make? If I'm just starting to walk, how are you going to tell me to walk straight, or how are you going to tell me to walk side to side, if I don't even know how to walk yet?

Nogueras: The Empowerment Zone process has been influenced by the outcomes of strategic events, such as the application process, preparation for implementation, the governing structure, and the monitoring and evaluation structure. What strategic events do you think will influence the Empowerment Zone process?

Rontos: I would say some of the strategic events were the meetings at Malcolm X. The city planned those meetings, and the community reacted to those meetings, and at one point, the community took over those meetings.

Nogueras: So you see that as a strategic event?

Rontos: I think the government planned those events in the way that they thought a meeting should be ran, which they thought would be strategic. The community, when they did take over the event, planned it also.

Nogueras: What happened? Can you tell me about that?

Rontos: Yes, because I was involved in the planning of that!

So it was like, "okay, the government's doing this, and we don't want the government just to . . . this is supposed to be bottoms-up, why aren't they consulting us? Why aren't we in the planning of this meeting? Why is it the way they want it to be?"

Nogueras: So you felt you were being shut out?

Rontos: Yes. I think what we did was we took over some meetings and said "Wait a minute, we don't want the government here. We want them to use their resources, but we don't want them to necessarily be there the whole time." I think they felt kind of like "Hey, wait a minute, we're trying to help, and you guys are shutting the door." And we were saying "When you help, you kind of take over" and "You're taking over everything, and I don't like that, either. Stop jamming your ideas down my throat." And you're rebelling. And you're saying "Well, I'm going to do it my way." So that's what happened.

Nogueras: Did you plan this?

Rontos: It was planned. There was talk of it. It was planned even during break.

Nogueras: Everybody had their roles...

Rontos: Everybody had their roles.

Nogueras: There are a number of different levels of participants in the EZ process. What levels were or are active, and to what extent?

Rontos: Well, grassroots organizing was worked in that from the beginning. I was also working as a zone resident. And what I was doing was representing an organization, Pilsen Neighbors, but I was also representing zone residents through the Pilsen Homeowner's Association. So I was looking at it from that perspective.

Nogueras: The Homeowner's Association?

Rontos: It's residents within the zone and even outside the zone. They are basically people that live within the community and the ward, that were just living here. I wanted to let them know what was happening, because I don't think zone residents really know what's happening.

Grassroots organizations—I kind of hate to see that used that way, because I don't think most organizations are grassroots anymore. I haven't seen a lot of that. I know Pilsen Neighbors isn't grassroots; it's institutionally-based. The 18th Street Development is not; it's business-based. Pilsen Resurrection also is church-based.

So what does grassroots mean? To me, grassroots means individual people. You're hitting the pavement. You're knocking on doors. You're finding out what's really going on. When you talk about institutions, then you have a perception of what's going on. And that's fine.

Nogueras: What was your role and responsibilities in the planning process?

Rontos: My role was in planning and working with grassroots people and working with organizations. I think also what responsibility that I took on was to build relationships with the other clusters, so that I wasn't just working within my own cluster, I was able to call on relationships with other cluster members as well. I think some of the responsibility I had to my organization that I was representing was coming back and making sure that they were part of the planning process, and that I was really representing them. At times I felt like I wasn't representing them, but representing my own ideas. Because they didn't feel that this was in their self-interests.

Nogueras: How would you describe the dynamics between and among government representatives, community, technical assistance providers, and residents during the planning process?

Rontos: I think for the first round we did pretty good. We managed to survive without killing each other. (laughs) There was a lot of city participation. The city was excellent in working with their different departments. I think that the state representative worked very well in representing the state. And the county, during the planning process I don't remember anybody from the county. And federally, only at special times were they called in.

Nogueras: Was that enough?

Rontos: I think maybe they could have been there a little more. I think that HUD, in Chicago, has been seen as some far-off entity. It could be as distant as Washington itself, even though it's a few blocks from City Hall. But the feeling is that it's that distant. And so I think HUD could have been, at the local level, should have and could have played a bigger role for the federal government.

I think that the community technical assistance providers worked well with the city and the state and federal government. I keep excluding the county because I never remember seeing county people there. I really can't remember them. Maybe they were sitting in the back row, quiet, watching everybody.

Nogueras: Do you feel like they should have been there?

Rontos: If they're going to do something, fine. But it's supposed to be city, state, county and federal. And if it's going to be city, state, county and federal, then I think that everybody should be there. I don't know what role the county is really going to provide. There might be some policy in taxes—property taxes—that we can use them and strategize more on the role they play and the opportunities that they bring to the table. Of course, the state is a big player; the federal government, of course. I think that the county is kind of a mystery to people, because we don't always know what the county has, or what services they can provide.

Nogueras: What adjustments need to be made for the planning process?

Rontos: Some of the adjustments that need to be made to the planning process are to have "people" there. I think what happens is some of the departments send out "technocrats."

Nogueras: What is that?

Rontos: Technical people. People that deal with numbers. People that deal with the technical stats. They're not really people persons, so they get in a room with grassroots people or organizations that assist people, and they don't know how to act or react. I think that sometimes you get so caught up in the policy that you don't understand, or you can't see beyond it. You know, you can't see the people that you're going to affect.

Nogueras: I hear you talking about the ability of the Department of Planning be represented by people persons. That seems to be very important to you.

Rontos: Yes, it's important to me because I think you need technical people that can do the specific writing, and dot the i's and make sure all the t's are crossed, but I think you also need a person who can really find out what the community needs. I don't necessarily think those are the same people. I try to do a little of both. But sometimes I have trouble crossing my t's and dotting my i's. I always have somebody else read over it!

I don't think that you can make good policy in a vacuum. I think you need to go out there and explore and see what's really going on. A lot of our technocrats are sitting in rooms without windows. You need the statistics to support your ideas, but you have to be realistic and know what's going on in the street. If you're not in the street, those statistics might say one thing, but the street says another. So you've got to make sure your streets and your statistics match.

Nogueras: What structures have been put into place at the government level and at the community level to facilitate implementation of Empowerment Zone activities?

Rontos: Well, I guess the structures include the Coordinating Council and its many levels of bureaucracy. I would say that's the structure. At the government level it would be the City Council, to implement the Empowerment Zone activities, but where it's really going to come down to is back here in the community with the aldermen, with the community organizations and people to implement those activities, and to make sure that they are going to happen in the manner that they were planned; in the good faith that they were planned. And that the people who don't should be held accountable. Structures —benchmarks— we have to put trust on the table. Without it, the rest doesn't matter much.

Nogueras: Are there any structures that you would consider new or innovative?

Rontos: I don't think what we have is innovative.

Nogueras: Are you talking about the Coordinating Council?

Rontos: Yes. I think it's like another board. I don't necessarily know what would be innovative. This is a board that makes recommendations that then go to the City Council. Like so many other boards it is bureaucratic. And at the same time, you have to look realistically at government. I mean, they're accountable for the money. So I wouldn't just hand it over to a Coordinating Council, unless I was handing that liability over too. The city is ultimately responsible for those funds. So I can understand why they want to have City Council approval as well.

Nogueras: So you think the structure of the Coordinating Council was just to defend, you know, this number here? Would you have structured it that way?

Rontos: You know what might be interesting, is if you had a mixture of government, and I mean elected officials, on the Coordinating Council. What might have been innovative is if you mixed the grassroots and the elected officials. I mean not just government bodies, but elected officials that had big stakes in this as well. Then have that be in the deciding place.

Nogueras: Right, now you see action.

Rontos: Yes, because right now it's the Coordinating Council that votes on it, then it goes to the City Council. And that's pretty much how other boards in the city work. If it would have been the other way, that could have been riskier. So I think the way it's set up is the best way. But if you wanted to go innovative, having a Council that made the decisions would have been interesting, to say the least.

Nogueras: Especially if you weren't working for the alderman, you were maybe a community person.

Rontos: Yes! I mean, it all depends. You've got to remember—different community groups don't always like each other. If you gave them the power, would they use it wisely?

There could have been a lot of wild things going on, so I think that the existing structure is good the way it is right now. I think it's a happy medium, but I don't think it's innovative.

Nogueras: In which ways should or will the rank-and-file community residents have input into the implementation of the Empowerment Zone activities?

Rontos: I don't know. I always get confused by this—by "community" and "residents", because like I said, most of this community, if you asked a regular guy in the street, "Are you in the Empowerment Zone?" I'm 95 percent sure he wouldn't even know what Empowerment Zone was.

I'm not talking just about our community residents, I'm talking about each cluster, anywhere. You knock on the door. "Hello. Do you know you live in the Empowerment Zone?" I bet you that they do not. Few people do know, and I think some residents that might be active within the community know. But you see just by voter turnout that people are apathetic. Also, big government programs such as this are looked at as Urban Renewal. That name carries connotations of displacement.

Nogueras: So you're saying that even before this question, it should be "Do people even know?"

Rontos: Yes. How will people react knowing they might have options and grant funds to change the look and feel of the community.

Nogueras: No, wait, go back to that! How do you think they would act?

Rontos: I tell you what, just as a community resident, just out of my own self-interest—what does this mean to me—I'd be pushing more, pressuring, saying, "I'm in the Zone! What benefits do I receive? If I'm going to be zoned, I want to get something!"

Something, because I mean really, what are residents going to get?

Nogueras: But you don't think that they're going to...

Rontos: I'm hoping!

Nogueras: I mean if it's explained, like they get jobs, or...

Rontos: I'm hoping that they do. Maybe I'm just being really pessimistic and reaching, but are people going to get jobs from this? What jobs are going to be created for them? Are they going to be high-level jobs? Are they going to be good jobs? Is there going to be a lot of training? What are we training these people for?

Nogueras: Wait, isn't that in the strategic plan? You know, I'm just asking, I don't know...

Rontos: Yes, it's in the strategic plan. What I'm saying is when you look at the Strategic Plan, when you look at everything—it's ideas and their abstract, I think when we were coming together we were training and were saying, "This is our dream. This is our vision. This is what we want." But when you're dreaming like that, and you're asking the rank-and-file of the community.... Are they going to have the same dream and the same vision as the people who dreamt this? Maybe there's different players. So they might have a little bit different dream.

I hope as time goes on we become clearer about our plans and implementation of them.

Nogueras: Well, what would you tell them?

 Rontos: I would tell them what the EZ means in social service block grant dollars. I would tell them what it means in community service. And then the community residents will turn around and say "Well, I don't use that. So what does it mean to me?"

Then you come back, and you say "OK, it means that your kid will be able to play in the Y." "But my kid can't play in the Y because he has to cross gang turf." And then I say "Well, we've got to plan for that. We're going to do something about public safety. We've got a strategic plan."

"Oh, yeah? Well, what's your strategic plan?"

"Well, I wasn't on that committee!" (laughs) "But I know we've got one!"

And then they say "Well, that's fine, but even if I could send my kid past there, I'm not home when they come home." "Well, why?" "Because I work two jobs."

"Well, we're working on jobs."

"Well, what does that mean to me?"

"Well, maybe we could get you a better job. And we're working on day care. And we're working on this..."

But you know, everybody's focused on just surviving the day! How am I supposed to focus on surviving for the next few years with some hundred million dollar project when people are more focused on day-to-day life and things like that?

I know organizations are representing their community. Do the community organizations represent the community residents? I don't know how much resident involvement there is and that debate is still going on within the Empowerment Zone and the cluster.

Nogueras: In which ways should the effects of the Empowerment Zone be measured?

Rontos: The Empowerment Zone should be measured by how much better of a job force we create, better education, and by the future of our children. That's how you're really going to be able to judge it— by the youth that's coming through the Empowerment Zone. Crime statistics will probably be lower. You'll see a better overall community presence. I think people will start taking pride. You'll see it, too, because it will be visible, but also measured by the improved quality of life for residents.

For example, I fix up my house, my neighbor sees me and starts fixing up his house, and so forth and so on. I think that kind of chain reaction you'll get from the Empowerment Zone, and that's what I would be measuring, rather than "We created x number of programs". I think those programs will only be if we're effective. Then they'll be successful.

I would say it's going to be long-term rather than short-term. These problems didn't happen overnight, so how can you alleviate them overnight?

Nogueras: Who do you think should do an evaluation?

Rontos: I think it should be various people. It should be community, it should be government, it should be all the kinds of people that comprise the Coordinating Council. I don't think it should be limited to the Coordinating Council, because, of course, they'll say "Yes! We did an excellent job!" But I think it should be various people. It should be some people interviewed on the street in the community. "Have you seen a change in your community? Have you seen something happen?" Go ask the librarian. Go ask the priest. Go ask somebody at church. Ask the housewife, community organizer, small business owners, aldermen, anyone who will impact or be impacted by the change of the EZ.

Nogueras: So that's something we could do, as researchers?

Rontos: Right! Go do a door-knocking; a random door-knocking, random call. "Did you notice anything new?" Ask the agencies, who are going to be impacted by receiving funds. Maybe interview some of their clients. But by whom? It can be done by a university. I think it should be done by students. I think this "By whom?" could be an employment opportunity. I think there could be a grant, which gives an opportunity for students, universities, and community residents to work together.

Nogueras: You're pointing out opportunities for whom? People in this community or in general?

Rontos: I think in each community, you could work with local educational entities to plan out questions that would give us feedback on the impact of EZs.

The Pilsen/Little Village cluster should have Pilsen/Little Village people calling around, and I don't think it should be done by the government. I don't think it should be community organizations making the evaluation, because I think they're all too involved in the process. It should be an outside entity.

But I don't think it should be somebody out of state. We have the resources within our neighborhood, so it should be something that benefits the community.

Nogueras: In your mind, how should quality of life issues be measured?

Rontos: Through quantitative analysis that can be researched by various methods, including surveys. We must also look at the intangibles, the experiences people have had, the growth process of the community, and the impact on the way we create policy, the inner workings of government.

Nogueras: How would you define reinventing government?

Rontos: I think government is okay. People just want to go back to the values of what it was originally. I don't think we're trying to reinvent government in a radical way, but people want to go back and even beyond the ideals of which this country was founded on. The words "reinventing government" scares people.

Nogueras: Why?

Rontos: Some residents, especially those who are immigrants, see reinventing government as an overthrow, a displacement of the system that exists. Even some government employees would like change within their departments and to cut levels of bureaucracy but fear the repercussions of being outspoken.

Reinventing government to some is an uncomfortable concept, but change is rarely accepted readily. Whenever we talk about redistributing power it will scare some and make others defensive.

As we go through the Empowerment Zone process, we will learn that reinventing government is a series of small changes, enhancing our government and its ability to work for the people. When we look back after ten years we will be able to judge the impact of reinventing government.

Nogueras: Do you think the Empowerment Zone is reinventing government?

Rontos: Yes, we have already begun by having intercommunication with various government entities, creating avenues for open discussions. As I said, the changes we make in reinventing government will be gradual. The impact will be in the long term.

Each step of the Empowerment Zone process and the hurdles we must face will help us reinvent government.

Nogueras: How would you define poverty alleviation?

Rontos: You know that there will always be poor. But the alleviation of poverty? That's a hard one. I don't even know how I would define it. I guess when we lessen the burden on people. When government really does what government is supposed to do, which is to step in where people can't necessarily take care of themselves. Step in and act, and not act in an aggressive manner, but act in a supportive manner. When we see that, we begin to educate instead of throwing money at the problem. Because if I just hand you five bucks, is that alleviating your poverty? It's alleviating it for today. It isn't going to alleviate it long-term. Poverty alleviation means that there has to be a long-term solution in helping people to get through their experience which has caused poverty—whether they've been born into it, or whatever the reason, our government and community has to help this person go step-by-step.

Another thing that's very important is the role of the philanthropic community. They are and will be a very important partner in creating support or alternative strategies for funding. They need to be more involved in the EZ process.

Nogueras: Has there been any philanthropic support?

Rontos: We've been trying to proposition the philanthropic community to come in and play a role, and they haven't. They want to take a more distanced approach and kind of see what's happening.

Nogueras: Is that what it is? Are they waiting?

Rontos: I think they're just doing a waiting game to see what happens.

Nogueras: What do you think they need to see?

Rontos: I think they need to see results.

Nogueras: Because that's what counts.

Rontos: Yes. Sometimes we need the money to get the results.

Nogueras: Catch 22.

Rontos: So how can I show you results if I don't have the money? Then the foundations say, "Well, you have the Empowerment Zone funds." Well, maybe that's not enough, because government funding is not enough. We need philanthropic support as well as sweat equity from the community. The Empowerment Zone is not one man's responsibility, it is all of ours, collectively, and we must all share the responsibilities of making it work.

So.... That's it!

Nogueras: Thanks.

References

Alkalimat, Abdul and associates. 1984. *Introduction To African American Studies: A People's College Primer*. Chicago: Twenty-First Century Publishers.

Alkalimat, Abdul and Doug Gills. 1989. *Harold Washington and the Crisis of Black Power*. Chicago: Twenty-First Century Publishers.

Anderson, Elijah. 1991. "Neighborhood Effects on Teenage Pregnancy." Pp. 375-98 in *The Urban Underclass*, edited by C. Jencks and P.E. Peterson. Washington, DC: Brookings Institution.

Berry, Jeffrey M., Kent E. Portnoy, and Ken Thomson. 1991. "The Political Behavior of Poor People." Pp. 357-74 in *The Urban Underclass*, edited by C. Jencks and P.E. Peterson. Washington, DC: Brookings Institution.

Betancur, John J. Betancur, Deborah E. Bennett, and Patricia A. Wright. 1991. "Effective Strategies for Community Economic Development." Pp. 142-168 in *Challenging Uneven Development: An Urban Agenda for the 1990s,* edited by Philip W. Nyden and Wim Wiewel. New Brunswick, NJ: Rutgers University Press.

Bobo, Lawrence and Franklin D. Gilliam Jr. 1990. "Race, Sociopolitical Participation, and Black Empowerment." *American Political Science Review* 84:377-93.

Brecher, Jeremy and Tim Costello. 1991. *Building Bridges: The Emerging Grassroots Coalition of Labor and Community*. New York: Monthly Review Press.

Carlson, Virginia L. and Nikolas C. Theodore. 1995. *Where Are the Jobs? Welfare Reform and Labor Market Reality*. DeKalb, IL: Northern Illinois University Center for Governmental Studies.

City of Chicago. 1994. *Empowering Chicago's Citizens, Volume I*. Application for EZ/EC designation submitted to the U.S. Department of Housing and Urban Development.

Clavel, Pierre and Wim Wiewel (eds.). 1991. *Harold Washington and the Neighborhoods: Progressive City Government in Chicago, 1983-1987*. New Brunswick, NJ: Rutgers University Press.

Cohen, Cathy J. and Michael C. Dawson. 1993. "Neighborhood Poverty and African American Politics." *American Political Science Review* 87:286-302.

Community Renewal Society. 1993. *Building Communities from Within*. Chicago: Community Renewal Society.

Crane, Jonathan. 1991a. "Effects of Neighborhoods on Dropping out of School and Teenage Childbearing." Pp. 299-320 in *The Urban Underclass*, edited by C. Jencks and P.E. Peterson. Washington, DC: Brookings Institution.

Crane, Jonathan. 1991b. "The Epidemic Theory of Ghettos and Neighborhood Effects on Dropping Out and Teenage Childbearing." *American Journal of Sociology* 96:1226-59.

Danziger, Sheldon and Peter Gottschalk, 1995, *America Unequal.* Cambridge: Harvard University Press.

Dye, Thomas R. and James Renick. 1981. "Political Power and City Jobs: Determinants of Minority Employment." *Social Science Quarterly* 62:475-86.

Eisinger, Peter K. 1982. "Black Employment in Municipal Jobs: The Impact of Black Political Power." *American Political Science Review* 76:380-92.

Federal Register. 1994. (January 18) 59:11.

Fisher, Robert and Joseph M. Kling (eds.). 1993. *Mobilizing the Community: Local Politics in the Era of the Global City*. Newbury Park, CA: Sage.

Gittell, Maryilyn, Janice Bockmeyer, Robert Lindsay, and Kathe Newman. 1996. *The Urban Empowerment Zones: Community Organizations and Community Capacity Building.* New York: Howard Samuels State Management and Policy Center of the Graduate School and University Center of the City University of New York.

Green, Roy (ed.). 1991. *Enterprise Zones: New Directions in Economic Development.* Newbury Park, CA: Sage Publications.

Guest, Avery M. and R.S. Oropesa. 1992. "Informal Social Ties and Political Activity in the Metropolis." *Urban Affairs Quarterly* 21:550-74.

Hanson, Susan and Geraldine Pratt. 1992. "Dynamic Dependencies: A Geographic Investigation of Local Labor Markets." *Economic Geography* 68:373-405.

Hanson, Susan and Geraldine Pratt. 1995. *Gender, Work, and Space.* London: Routledge.

Hinz, Greg. 1994. "Moving Violation." *Chicago* 43:21-23.

Holzer, Harry J. 1987. "Informal Job Search and Black Youth Unemployment." *American Economic Review* 77:446-52.

Kasinitz, Philip and Jan Rosenberg. 1994. "Missing the Connection: Social Isolation and Employment on the Brooklyn Waterfront."

Working Paper from the Michael Harrington Center, Queens College, City University of New York.

King, A. Thomas. 1975. "The Demand for Housing: Integrating the Roles of Journey-to-Work, Neighborhood Quality, and Prices." Pp. 451-84 in *Household Production and Consumption*. N.E. Terleckyj (ed.). New York: Columbia University Press.

Kretzmann, John and Bryan McKnight. 1993. *Building Communities from the Inside Out*. Evanston, IL: Northwestern University Center For Urban Affairs and Policy Research.

LaVeist, Thomas A. 1992. "The Political Empowerment and Health Status of African-Americans: Mapping a New Territory." *American Journal of Sociology* 97:1080-95.

Marable, Manning. 1985. *Black American Politics: From the Washington Marches to Jesse Jackson*. New York: Verso.

Marable, Manning. 1986. *How Capitalism Underdeveloped Black America: Problems in Race, Political Economy and Society*. Boston: South End Press.

Massey, Doug and Nancy Denton. 1993. *American Apartheid: Segregation and the Making of the Underclass*. Cambridge, MA: Harvard University Press.

McDonald, John. 1993, "Tax expenditures for local economic Growth: an Econometric Evaluation of the Illinois Enterprise Zone Program," *Public Budgeting and Financial Management* 5:477-505.

Mier, Robert. 1993. *Social Justice and Local Development Policy.* Newbury Park, CA: Sage Publications.

Milbrath, Lester. 1981. "Political Participation." *Handbook of Political Behavior* 4:197-240.

NCI Research. 1995. *Metropolitan Chicago Skill-Based Labor Market Information System and Quality Assurance Program: A Demonstration Program for Transportation and Distribution Occupations.* Chicago: Chicago United.

Nyden, Philip W. and Wim Wiewel (eds.). 1991. *Challenging Uneven Development: Toward an Urban Agenda for the 1990s.* New Brunswick, NJ: Rutgers University Press.

President's Community Empowerment Board. 1995. *Building Communities Together: Urban Empowerment Zones and Enterprise Communities.* Washington, DC: U.S. Department of Housing and Urban Development.

Ranney, David C. and John J. Betancur. 1992. "Labor-Force-Based Development: A Community-Oriented Approach to Targeting Job Training and Industrial Development." *Economic Development Quarterly* 6:286-96.

Rawls, John, 1971, *A Theory of Justice*. Cambridge: Harvard University Press.

Skogan, Wesley G. 1990. *Disorder and Decline*. New York: Free Press.

Theodore, Nikolas C. and Virginia L. Carlson. Forthcoming, 1997. "Targeting Job Opportunities for the Hard to Employ: Developing Measures of Local Employment." *Economic Development Quarterly*.

Theodore, Nikolas C. and D. Garth Taylor. 1991. *The Geography of Opportunity: The Status of African Americans in the Chicago Area Economy*. Chicago: Chicago Urban League.

U.S. Department of Commerce, Bureau of the Census. 1992. *Census of Population and Housing, 1990: Summary Tape File 3*. Washington, DC: U.S. Bureau of the Census.

U.S. Department of Housing and Urban Development. 1994. *Building Communities Together*. Washington, DC: U.S. Government Printing Office.

United Way of Chicago. *Assessing Chicago's Human Needs, Series IV: Report of the Needs Assessment Committee*. Chicago: United Way of Chicago.

United Way of Chicago. 1993. *Assessing Chicago's Human Needs, Series V: Report of the Needs Assessment Committee.* Chicago: United Way of Chicago.

United Way of Chicago. 1994. *Assessing Chicago's Human Needs, Series VI: Report of the Needs Assessment Committee.* Chicago: United Way of Chicago.

Wilson, William Julius. 1987. *The Truly Disadvantaged: The Inner City, the Underclass, and Public Policy.* Chicago: University of Chicago Press.

About the Contributors

Michael Bennett is the Executive Director of DePaul University's Egan Urban Center and a co-Principal Investigator for the National Empowerment Zone Action Research Project. Previously, Dr. Bennett was Assistant Professor at the Jane Addams School of Social Work, a Great Cities Institute Scholar, and a Faculty Associate in the Center for Urban Economic Development at the University of Illinois at Chicago. Dr. Bennett is also a former Vice President of Shorebank Corporation and President of the Shorebank affiliate, the Neighborhood Institute. He has broad-ranging interests and experience in community and economic development which began with his early work in Ohio as a youth organizer and as Executive Director of an anti-poverty community action agency.

Kathy Feingold received her Masters of Urban Planning and Policy from the University of Illinois at Chicago in May of 1997. She worked as a researcher with the National Empowerment Zone Action Research Project from January of 1995 to September of 1996, focusing primarily on the Chicago and New York Empowerment Zones. She most recently worked at the City of Chicago's Department of Planning and Development as part of the Chicago Empowerment Zone's administrative staff.

Douglas Gills is Assistant Professor of community development in the Urban Planning and Policy Program and the Center for Urban Economic Development in the College of Urban Planning and Public Affairs at the University of Illinois at Chicago. He was a 1996 UIC Great Cities

Fellow, the former Deputy Director of the Kenwood Oakland Community Organization, a current Board member of the Chicago Algebra Project, and a co-founder of several education and community development associations and coalitions in Chicago, including the Community Workshop on Economic Development, The Neighborhood Capital Budget Group, and the Policy Research Action Group. He is a social action researcher who has participated in the design and implementation of Chicago's Empowerment Zone initiative. He is a co-Principal Investigator of the National Empowerment Zone Action Research Project.

Cedric Herring is Professor of Sociology, Interim Director of the Institute for Research on Race and Public Policy at the University of Illinois at Chicago, co-Principal Investigator of the National Empowerment Zone Action Research Project, and a former Great Cities Institute Scholar. Dr. Herring has published extensively in social policy, political sociology, labor force issues and policies, inequality, and the sociology of Black Americans. He is the author of *Splitting the Middle: Political Alienation, Acquiescence, and Activism,* and editor of *African Americans and the Public Agenda: The Paradoxes of Public Policy.* He is Past President of the Association of Black Sociologists.

Noah Temaner Jenkins (Masters of Urban Planning and Policy, University of Illinois at Chicago 1995) is the Project Coordinator for the National Empowerment Zone Action Research Project at DePaul University's Monsignor John J. Egan Urban Center. In this capacity she formulates research design, analyzes public policy, develops and writes grant proposals and reports, coordinates local and national research, supervises student researchers, and performs research. She is also senior editor of the project's nationally recognized newsletter, *EZ Exchange*. She has also conducted research and analysis of economic development issues at UIC's Center for Urban Economic Development and Great Cities Institute and the United Way of Chicago, and is familiar with educational issues from her experiences as an instructor for English as a Second Language and GED tutoring programs. Ms. Jenkins is a member of the Board of Directors for the Chicago Counseling and Psychotherapy Center.

John F. McDonald is Professor of Economics and Finance and Director of the Center for Urban Real Estate at the University of Illinois at Chicago, where he has been a member of the faculty since 1971. He served as President of the Illinois Economic Association during 1993-94. His most recent book is *Fundamentals of Urban Economics*, which was published by Prentice-Hall in 1997.

Javier Nogueras is a lifelong resident, homeowner, and businessman in the Humboldt Park area of Chicago. He is currently the chair of the Humboldt Park Empowerment Partnership. He has been involved in some major organizing movements, including one of the largest Hispanic voter registration drives in Chicago and historic victories against the Alcohol and tobacco industry.

Mark Sendzik is a PhD candidate in the Public Policy Analysis Program at the University of Illinois at Chicago with a concentration in urban sustainable development. His background includes supervising disaster relief operations and providing assistance to homeless families.

Anna Marie Schuh has worked for the federal government for over thirty years, primarily in the human resource management area. In her current position as Assistant Director for Effectiveness with the U.S. Office of Personnel Management, she is responsible for the federal government's research and demonstration efforts in the personnel area. This responsibility includes working with agencies to develop demonstration projects, conduct public hearings, and ensure post project evaluation. She also is a University of Illinois at Chicago graduate student and expects to defend her PhD dissertation soon. Her research involves the use of a policy window model and civil service change data to surface differences in administrative and legislative policy making.

Michelle L. Story-Stewart received her Bachelor of Arts Degree in Economics from Northwestern University in 1992. She received her Master of Arts Degree in Economics from the University of Illinois at Chicago in 1994. Currently, she is a PhD candidate in Public Policy Analysis in the Urban Planning Program at the University of Illinois at Chicago. Her dissertation research focuses on citizen and community involvement in the design and implementation of the Empowerment Zone Strategic Plan.

Nikolas Theodore is Project Director in the Research and Planning Department of the Chicago Urban League. His work examines the operation of low-wage labor markets in Chicago. Current research uses a combination of secondary data sources, resident surveys, and firm interviews to assist job training agencies and to inform community planning activities. The main focus of this work is to identify employment opportunities that meet the needs of residents in economically disadvantaged neighborhoods.

Wanda White is currently the Director of Development Initiatives for the Chicago Housing Authority. She is the former Executive Director of the Community Workshop on Economic Development (CWED). A Former Deputy Commissioner for Chicago's Economic Development Department serving three Chicago Mayors, Ms. White maintains an active role in community development and technical assistance to individuals and organizations on community development through her active participation on several Chicago not-for-profit boards and advisory committees.